Also by George Sheehan

Dr. Sheehan on Running

Dr. Sheehan's Medical Advice

Running and Being: The Total Experience

This Running Life

How to Feel Great 24 Hours a Day
  (published in paperback as *Dr. Sheehan on Fitness*)

Personal Best

Running to Win

Going the Distance

Going the

Distance

One Man's Journey to the End of His Life

George Sheehan, M.D.

Introduction by Robert Lipsyte

Villard ❦ New York

For Mary Jane

Library of Congress Cataloging-in-Publication Data

Sheehan, George.
Going the distance : one man's journey to the end of his life / by George Sheehan.
    p. cm.
  ISBN 0-679-44843-8
  1. Death—Psychological aspects. 2. Sheehan, George. 3. Cancer—Patients—
United States.
I. Title.
BF789.D4S475 1996
155.9'37—dc20   95-41384

Printed in the United States of America on acid-free paper

98765432

First Edition

Book design by Nora Sheehan

Introduction by Robert Lipsyte

EORGE SHEEHAN'S MIND ALWAYS outran us, swept past on the straightaway, invariably took me on the curve. The first time was a few hours before the 1968 Boston Marathon. I was trolling through the dressing area for characters to write about. The marathon seemed like aberrational behavior, certainly worthy of long-distance irony. I picked him out of the pack, I thought, but that was a secret gift of his, drawing you to him with that haunted, hawkish look. He read me by the second or third uninformed question, and grabbed me forever by casually suggesting that I try to view the race as a Greek tragedy.

"There is hubris and there is nemesis," he said, fussing with his shirt. "The beginning of the course is downhill and everyone is charged up. They run too fast and their pride destroys them."

Thanks for the lead to the column, O Socrates in sneakers. But, of course, he was much more than that. A few years later, he wanted to know what I was doing for what was left of my body, and before I could mumble excuses he said that not everyone was built for running, that cycling and swimming were very good, too, that there was no One Way for trying to get the most out of your life. If I did feel like trying to, ahem, jog, I should start very slow, wear cheap stuff, maybe old Hush Puppies, and even a ski mask so the neighbors won't laugh. He told me to listen to my body, not to other people. It was liberating advice in a rising time of fitness fascism. He gave me permission to do my best, and he gave me advance promise that if it was my best, it would always be good enough. I'm still going slow, but I've never stopped, thanks to George.

The last time I saw him, in the summer of 1993, he casually suggested that I try to view his dying as a blood sport, like bullfighting. "The bull, of course, is death," he said, "and I am defending myself, dancing with death, creating this beautiful aesthetic. The blood sports show us that death is not defeat."

Thanks again for the lead. But then he got to the grit, as he always did given enough road, and he talked about the morphine he was now taking twice a day, how important it was to stay ahead of needless agony. He said he was beginning to think that "this whole drug thing" was blown out of proportion. "More people die from gunshots than overdoses," he said, his blue eyes bright with recent research. He wondered why doctors were so afraid of giving people drugs. What's so terrible about elderly addicts if the alternative is mind-numbing pain? Are doctors hidebound? Is it about control? He said that thinking about this was leading him toward a reevaluation of himself as a person and as a physician. Who knows how far he would have run with that if he hadn't run out of road four months later.

Keeping an eye on him for twenty-five years, as his public persona changed from George Sheehan, M.D., to Doc Sheehan to George, was an education by example; he never stopped seeking and growing and refining himself, usually for the better. He became less snappish as he grew older, more willing to give slack. As the world embraced him, he began to embrace back, although always in his own cool, measured way. He was never a high-fiver or hugger. His spirituality was idiosyncratic enough that there was room for yours, even if you didn't know you had any spirituality until he showed you your own soul. His importance in the world of physical fitness—actually, in the world of total self-improvement—was immeasurable.

George was not only an original, he was the anti-Schwarzenegger. They both came to acclaim, remember, in the so-called Me Decade, when Yippies and Yuppies and Boomers were all trying to grab a pole on a merry-go-round turning mean. The quickest, the seemingly most accessible grip was on one's own flesh. Re-form your body, control your most immediate environment. Arnold showed us how you could be pumped up into a huge, fabulously wealthy juggernaut of consumption. George showed us how to pare down to the basic humanity of peace and personal best.

Other people may have made more money on the jogging craze, but George made more sense out of it and widened its moral purpose, which was not to live longer (to run more?) but to live better, to have more energy and self-worth and clarity for all the more important things to do in life than run. This passion of Saint George could have come only from a born-again, which he was. George was one of fourteen siblings, and probably found his solitude as a high school and college runner. He played racquet games as an adult until he broke his hand at forty-three and began running again. As the sometimes distant father of twelve who rarely ran with his kids, he might have begun this as another way of being alone. He told me in 1968 that he ran at midday because "when you give up lunch, you're only giving up companionship." Ten years later, he was rarely alone.

He was angry at getting cancer, but not surprised. He had never said he would live longer, only better. Once, he had been saved from drowning in a riptide by a sudden wave; that became a premonition that his death would be slow.

George made his death his own, as he had made his life his own, the object of research, metaphor, and tinkering. He *flirted* with death, experimenting with the dosage of Gn-RH, the hypothalamic hormone he took to block his body's production of testosterone. Prostate cancer rides to metastasy on currents of male hormone, and the Gn-RH performed a chemical castration. He was delighted, he told me in a phone conversation. For the first time in his life, he said, his mind was truly clear.

"I am the eye in the sky now," he crowed, "and I see how ludicrous men are, acting out a script written by a gland in their bodies. It's all testosterone. The only thing that protects us against it is good manners."

But that was the philosopher talking, not the jock. George was competitive, even if he was competing against his only truly worthy adversary, himself; how else to explain that fierce will to win, to do better, to set records? Chemical castration might be holding back the cancer, but it was also holding back George. He needed the testosterone to run faster. So he fiddled with the dosage in the daily Gn-RH injections, sometimes skipping them altogether when a race was coming up. He was willing to whittle days off the end of his life so he could be at his best. Some say George was not perfect. I say he was better than that: he was true to himself.

The jock in George was not the only competitor. The writer was hungry to score. I told him once that no one who ran faster than he did could write better, and no one who wrote better could run faster. He smiled, but his eyes told me he was patronizing me. George hated the idea of anyone beating him. And, of course, who else but George could pack gastrointestinalia and Ortega y Gasset in the same graph, could find more portents in a footfall than did Emily Dickinson? Sometimes I thought that his references to Thoreau and Rilke and Nietzche and the James boys were less to buttress his thoughts than to show the world that the old-timers were plugged in too. George knew he didn't really need the Greeks to help him teach us to "spend your life learning how to live."

He was still learning that the last time I saw him, four months before he died. We would talk again, but I remember that day's talk best. It was a day of gorgeous life, the sun splashing off the ocean and the beach, filling his living room. Beneath the windows, joggers huffed by. How many of them had he set on the road? He wasn't interested in dwelling on the past, or on other people's ambitions.

"I have come to believe," he said, with a hint of edge, "that you shouldn't write about the marathon unless you've run it and you shouldn't write about cancer unless you've got it. And you shouldn't write about death unless you're dying. Now, this book I'm doing, it's going to be good. But the epilogue is going to be a problem."

The book is good; turn the page and find out for yourself. And no problem on the epilogue, George. We are your epilogue, all the people to whom you gave courage and inspiration, all the people who want to say, again, thank you.

Contents

Introduction by Robert Lipsyte   vii

Preface   xvii

Discovery   3

A Healthy Way to Be Ill   29

Running with (and Against) Cancer   45

The Physician and the Patient   69

My Family and Me   101

A Little Help from My Friends   123

The Cancer Is Winning   139

Facing the Future   153

A Blood Sport   175

Epilogue   183

Preface

SOMEONE ASKED SARAH, OUR MOST GRE-
garious daughter, how I was facing terminal cancer. "Oh, he loves it," she said.
"He writes about it in his columns, he
talks about it in his lectures."

The truth is often blunt and to the
point. Without my cancer, my days would have the sameness that I now wish to escape. Cancer is like everything
else in life—an experience. And the root word indicates
experiment—*peril.* I have to explore death to the very
edge, just as I have done with my running.

My writing, my speeches need new material if they are

to interest me or others. Otherwise, I have only the alternative of a few years ahead with people astounded that at my age I still can run and finish ahead of people much younger.

Anything worthwhile must come from my own experience. This book is about what dying actually means to a person undergoing it. This book is also a communion with others experiencing dying. And it is an evaluation of my life, some estimate of my success in becoming the self I was meant to be.

Going the Distance

*At times my father could be brutally honest. He'd say
things you wished he hadn't said because you would be left
thinking about them for years. One such time was when I
was a young adult and he told me that of all his
roles—son, brother, doctor, husband, father—he felt he
was the weakest at being a father.*

*Sometimes I agreed with him—when I yearned for a
father who would come home for dinner and stay home all
weekend, or when he left my mother and the family to
search for new experiences in his life. But most of the time
I loved him so much I wanted to prove him wrong.*

ANN

But I have promises to keep,
And miles to go before I sleep. . . .

ROBERT FROST

Discovery

NOW THAT I AM SEVENTYSOMEthing, I read the ancients with a new understanding. Seneca and Epictetus make great good sense. Plato and Plutarch and Aristotle, I am learning, knew what they were writing about. Their message rings down through the centuries: Spend your life learning how to live.

For the Greeks the supreme art was the art of existence. Every moment of the day, every action followed a plan. Life was made through the techniques of living. And that was their number one task. "It is never too early or late," says Epictetus, "to care for the well-being of the soul."

Early or late, however, it is a full-time job. "Taking care of the self is not a rest cure," writes Michel Foucault in discussing Greek life. "There is the care of the body to consider, health regimens, physical exercise, the carefully measured satisfaction of needs. And then the meditations, the reading, the notes one takes on books, or on conversations one has heard, the recollection of truths."

And this is but the beginning. I must add a retreat within myself, talks with a guide or confidant, letters to solicit or give advice. In Foucault's words, "No less than an entire activity of speaking and writing in which the work on oneself and communication with others are linked together."

This work goes on daily. Attention has to be focused continually on the body. Again Foucault offers us Seneca and Marcus Aurelius as examples of this preoccupation: "Fear of excess, economy of regimen, being on the alert for disturbances, detailed examination of dysfunction, the taking into account of all factors (seasons, climate, diet, mode of living) that might disturb the body and, through it, the soul."

Disturbances of the soul are more difficult to detect than those of the body. "The insidious thing about the diseases of the soul," claims Plutarch, "is that they pass unnoticed or even that one can mistake them for virtues (anger for courage, amorous passion for friendship, envy for emulation, cowardice for prudence)."

The response of the ancient philosophers to possible deviations from our proper course was the development of the techniques of self-knowledge. This life I am now leading, therefore, must be subjected to constant examination. The first part of that survey is called "testing procedures." This process is designed to establish a supremacy over oneself—and thereby to do without unnecessary items and acquire important virtues.

Next comes the habit of scrutinizing the day: first in the morning when plans are made, then in the evening to see how one has done and how one could do better. This custom of Pythagoras is not so much an examination of conscience as it is a matter of setting up a game plan and then noting what went wrong with it.

Finally, the Greeks set great store by living according to your belief. That, in their thinking, led to the happy life. This principle puts great emphasis on what is under one's own control—because to a great degree that constitutes the self. Concern for anything beyond what you can control is nonproductive.

These practices reflect the Greeks' total involvement in the process of becoming a person. They give a density to every day. Anything that happens can cause me to be better or worse. Each day holds the ever-present possibility of either an advance or a retreat. Life becomes an investigation of truth ended only by death.

When I entered this Grecian phase of my life, I never suspected how difficult it would be. The easy rhythm of my usual days seemed to satisfy everyone's prescription for the good life. I was fit, my mental capabilities were adequate, my emotional profile was within normal limits. And if I wasn't quite certain about my ultimate destination, who is?

I thought of myself as a veteran, experienced in life, ready to give advice to another generation. Now I see that the ancients would look on me as a mere recruit, fresh from basic training. Any Greek would suspect that I was a blind and deaf tenant of my body. Any Greek would know my mind had been penned up in a corral, never suspecting the great vistas that awaited it. And it would be clearly evident that I had never subjected my life to the rigorous analysis Socrates would force on a pupil.

Fortunately, even at seventysomething it is never too late. And there is one thing the Greeks made plain. I already possess everything I need. It becomes a matter of making actual what is only potential. And doing it one day at a time.

· · ·

TO MANY PEOPLE GROWING OLD SEEMS LIKE THE endgame in chess: life winding down in a series of small moves with lesser pieces. As I age I have discovered this is not true. I am not an elderly king stripped of my powers, reduced to a ragtail army of pawns. My life is not a defensive struggle of restricted options. Growing old is a game of verve and imagination and excitement.

The aging game is chess at its best. The opening gambit may have been made long ago. The responses long since set in motion. Some pieces have indeed been lost. But the board is still filled with opportunity. The outcome is not now a matter of strength, although that still remains, but of faith and courage, hope and wisdom.

The aging game is a sport for which childhood and youth and maturity are no more than a preparation. Its scope comes as a surprise. It expands my life at a time when I expected it to diminish. It demands an excellence that no longer seemed necessary. It asks me to surpass what I did at the peak of my powers. Age will not accept second best.

In the aging game I must be all I ever was and am yet to be. What has gone before is no more than a learning period. A breaking in. Life, someone has said, is boot camp. If it is, age is the combat for which I was trained. Now I must take this person I have become and make each new day special. I must make good on the promise of every dawn I am privileged to see.

Life goes from a minor to a major key. The game builds to a climax. Every move assumes importance. One feels like a virtuoso. The gifts we have been given, the powers that empower us, the marvels that make us marvelous are evident as never before. The truth is that we have lost nothing. The problem is not that I am less than I was when I was young, it is that I am not more. It is past time to become my own person. That is why the aging game begins with the awareness of one's need to grow and expand in every sphere of one's existence.

One also learns that honesty is the only policy. As I age I find less and less need to dissemble. I have little difficulty looking truth in the eye and admitting it. Lies and deception are time-consuming, and time becomes essential.

Time is what shapes the aging game. The clock and the calendar force me to make a move. Age does not permit the dallying with options that characterize youth. A labyrinth might be sport to the young. It brings panic to the old. My goal must be clear. The project outlined. The requirements understood. I must decide—if not this way, then there is no other way.

Fortunately, I find this commitment no problem. I accept the game and the goals I have developed in those formative years. I enjoy the self I have become. I no longer desire to be what I am not. My dissatisfaction is only in my failure to accomplish what is clearly attainable.

Such revelations frequently come late in life. They may arrive after decades of going in the wrong direction. I have a letter from a seventy-four-year-old woman who had just run the Honolulu Marathon. "I have felt great ambivalence because by nature I seem to be a selfish person involved in understanding myself," she writes. "I picked social work as a career and was never really happy with it. I was much more interested in a variety of creative contemplative activities—dance, print making, poetry, all things hard to make a living at. Now I am retired and my own person. It is a new and wonderful life."

This woman is a master at the aging game, in part because she brings to it the enthusiasm and zest and urgency that had been bottled up during those long years of social work. She is finally a united self.

I continue to strive for that state. On the other side of my chessboard of life is a self with different interests. I look at this mirror image of me and see opposite tendencies. My alter ego sits there attempting to destroy my game, to block the forays of my knights, the hammering of my rooks, the sweeps of my bishops. This contented self wants to play the sacrifice game. This lesser "me" is

playing for a draw, letting the clock run down and looking to the postgame comforts, rest and relaxation and retirement.

There are, you can see, two ways to play the aging
game.

S HEEHAN, PAY ATTENTION!" HOW OFTEN I HEARD
that admonition in school. The order that I put
my daydreams aside and join in the lesson being
taught. The teacher demanding my presence, asking that
I be not merely "here," but actively engaged in the subject
at hand.

But there I sat, my eyes glazed, my ears unhearing, all
senses on hold. No longer aware of what was going on
around me or indeed even where I was. My imagination
was at the controls as I journeyed into my inner space.

The teacher's task is to circumvent this escape. Teaching, William James once said, is the insertion of a creative
mind between a fact and a pupil. Nothing can be accomplished without undivided attention from both parties to
this undertaking.

Both in life and in school we must pay attention. Daydreams come true only when preceded by the serious
mental effort that learning requires. Yet what I did as a
student I have continued through my adult life. I am off
in a world of my own making.

At times I am pulled up short. Some inexcusable ignorance, some error in judgment, an instance of pure
cowardice, a neglected friendship, the acceptance of indo-
lence, and suddenly I hear that inner voice: "Sheehan, pay
attention!"

I realize, then, that I have stopped learning. I am no
longer present. I am preoccupied with the inconsequen-
tial. I miss the significant. I am daydreaming while life is
trying to teach me how to live. I would learn from experience but I fail to notice I have had an experience. I am
absent when the day's events spell out insights on the
human condition.

It is no excuse to say I am a philosopher; a philosophy
does not develop a priori, it comes into being a posteri-
ori—after the event. We shape ourselves and our philo-
sophies through observing and understanding the
occurrences of the day. If philosophy is, as someone
has said, "disguised autobiography," we must live it to
write it.

"The world's a stage," said Shakespeare. And more
than that. It is the school where life, the great teacher,
goes over the lesson for today. Yet we sit there, or at least I
do, and look out the window thinking of other worlds.

"Sheehan, pay attention!" If only this Japanese miracle
on my wrist would intone that phrase on the hour. It
would bring me back to the living, back to using my five

senses, back to extracting the "how" and especially the "why" of what is happening around me. Teaching myself, because now I am both student and teacher, that the world is filled with miraculous things and none more miraculous than we humans who populate it.

Now, more than ever, I want to know. Know how the world works. But even more I want to know why. Why I am here. Why I must die. I can make this search in several ways. I can retire into myself and think about it. Or I can go day by day seeing the world as my schoolroom and paying very strict attention.

W E WERE MEANT TO BE FIELD ANIMALS," writes the great cardiologist Paul Dudley White, "to rise with the sun, to be out in the open air, to be always active and to eat only when we are hungry." Living at the beach house is just such a life. I have become, if not a field animal, an aborigine. At the shore there is no past or future, no was or will be. Time simply is. I become part of nature, of sun and sand and sea. My body is now governed by the cycles of dark and light, of eating and drinking, of activity and rest.

Here at the ocean's edge I can feel, as the theologian Paul Tillich said, "the ebb and flow of the universe." Even more apparent is the ebb and flow of the human animal. The body takes charge. This is an existence that begins in the senses and is guided by instinct. My body determines when I rise, when I eat, when I nap, when I am in motion, when I sleep.

We have no alarm clocks to announce the day, and need none. I am awakened by the splendid light of the rising sun filling my room. It floods through the windows and the open door of the upper porch. And its reflection off the water shines on the ceiling over the bed. What a morning!

I am impelled to action. I am out of bed, into a bathing suit, and plunging into the surf in the space of time I might ordinarily spend deliberating on whether or not to get up. There is no escaping this clarion call. The day is here. All's right with the world.

The ocean at dawn may be at high or low tide. But my waking body, now filled with the energy stored in sleep, is always at flood. I am like a dam ready to burst. All I need is the sunlight to set me in motion. Thus begins the systole and diastole, the effort and repose of daily life at the beach. It makes for days similar to what psychiatrist Robert Jay Lifton enjoyed at Cape Cod, "with the incomparable dunes and the magnificent ocean; the rhythm of days and nights, the unparalleled purity of work and play devoid of interruptions and irrelevancies and necessities."

The day at the beach house is spent in living. It is an intense immersion into the language of the body. There is an intent cocking of one's ear to hear what is going on inside. To learn the instructions for a human being. And the life that results is much like the idyllic life of the child. It is filled with action and intensity and enthusiasm and equally filled with rest and relaxation and sleep. Living here is a remembrance of things past. It is Thoreau's thought relived: "In youth before I lost my senses, I can remember when I was all alive, and inhabited my body with inexpressible satisfaction; both its weariness and refreshment were sweet to me."

There is time yet for all of us to relive that time.

WHY DO I RUN? I HAVE WRITTEN OVER THE years of the benefits I receive from running. Enumerated the physical and mental changes. Listed the emotional and spiritual gains. Charted the improvement that has taken place in my person and my life. What I have not emphasized is how transient these values and virtues are.

With just a little thought, however, it should be evident that physical laws parallel those of the mind and the spirit. We know that the effects of training are temporary. I cannot put fitness in the bank. If inactive, I will detrain in even less time than it took me to get in shape. And since my entire persona is influenced by my running program, I must be constantly in training. Otherwise the sedentary life will inexorably reduce my mental and emotional well-being.

So, I run each day to preserve the self I attained the day before. And coupled with this is the desire to secure the self yet to be. There can be no letup. If I do not run I will eventually lose all I have gained—and my future with it.

Maintenance was a favorite topic of Eric Hoffer. It made the difference, said the former longshoreman, between a country that was successful and one that failed. However magnificent the achievement, without constant care the result was decay.

I know that experience intimately. There is nothing more brief than the laurel. Victory is of the moment. It must be followed by another victory and then another. I have to run just to stay in place.

Excellence is not something attained and put in a trophy case. It is not sought after, achieved and, thereafter, a steady state. It is a momentary phenomenon, a rare conjunction of body, mind, spirit at one's peak. Should I come to that peak I cannot stay there. I must start each day at the bottom and climb to the top. And then beyond that peak to another and yet another.

Through running I have learned what I can be and do. My body is now sensitive to the slightest change. It is particularly aware of any decline or decay. I can feel this lessening of the "me" that I have come to think of myself.

Running has made this new me. Taken the raw material and honed it and delivered it back ready to do the work of a human being. I run so I do not lose the me I was yesterday and the me I might become tomorrow.

IN 1985, I WAS IN DALLAS TO GIVE A TALK AT A FITness festival. The day before, I had challenged Dr. Ken Cooper's treadmill and had broken the record for my age group, sixty-five-plus.

Afterward, as I lay on a table recovering, I felt as if I were joining the immortals. Despite my age, I had performed in the ninety-ninth percentile of the seventy thousand tests done at the Aerobics Center.

Then Cooper announced he was going to give me a physical examination. Before I could protest, I was stripped down and experiencing what anyone experiences in a visit to the doctor. The results of this examination (which led to tests that would eventually discover a malignancy) made me face my own mortality.

It hardly seemed possible that only a week before I had been fretting about the normal vicissitudes of life—running, for one. My race times had deteriorated over the past year. I had rarely thought of my aging before; now I was becoming preoccupied with my age. I had reached a point where no amount of training made me improve. My writing was boring me. Many times before, I had thought that I was all written out. This time it was really true. When I took on a subject, I found I had done it before—and better. No phrases appeared that did not land with a thud and then lie there lifeless.

But I had known all these defeats in the past. The cycles came and went, as fundamental as the seasons and as unchangeable. I should have made up my mind to treat them as a fact of life, to accept that even champions have their slumps. The best of all know the worst of times—and use those experiences when the bright, beautiful, productive days return.

The news I received in Dallas gave me that different perspective. Even before the results of the tests were in, my future had been decided. My life had been unalterably changed.

Psychologist Abraham Maslow called the years subsequent to his heart attack his "postmortem life." It was a time he viewed as a gift: hours of appreciating what he had taken for granted, days used in the best possible way.

The notion of a postmortem has even more implications. Postmortems are done to ascertain the cause of death. A postmortem life should uncover what was wrong with the previous one. How should I have lived that I would now be content? Why did I not bear my fruit, bring my message, reap my harvest? What became of the "I" that was to be? The questions multiply. One's life, which had previously seemed well ordered, is seen to be neither ordered nor well.

Each New Year's Day we think on these failures in the past. We make resolutions about the future. What has happened to me has made this traditional practice tremendously important. I see clearly that my life depends on what I decide to do with it.

So much of life passes without our being in it at all. For me, this is especially true about my relationships with other people. I have not entered their lives, nor they mine.

At about the same time as my cancer appeared, I heard a former United States senator tell of his reaction on learning he had a malignancy. He had resigned from the Senate, but not for medical reasons. He could have finished his term satisfactorily, but his reason for leaving was the heightened awareness his malignancy had given him. He had reexamined his life and then determined to live it in a different way. He discovered that the people in his life were more important than his career.

The big question is how one should live one's life. Writer and philosopher Miguel de Unamuno had this answer: "Our greatest endeavor must be to make ourselves irreplaceable—to make the fact that each one of us is unique and irreplaceable, that no one can fill the gap when we die, a practical truth."

After receiving my news, I learned I could do that—make that fact a practical truth. I will be irreplaceable. I will leave a gap. Each day, family and friends have affirmed my importance to them.

When you are between the sword and the stone, you know who you want standing beside you. When time is short, it becomes obvious who the essential people are in your life.

People who know they have cancer have a motto: "Make every day count." I have done that. What I have not done is make every person count. My life has been filled with the best of me. What it has not been filled with is the best of others.

I now know that Robert Frost was right. I have promises to keep, and miles to go before I sleep.

I HAVE MADE MAJOR MISTAKES IN MY LIFETIME—BUT none equal to this one. I gave no thought to being checked for cancer. I knew better. I had virtually eliminated the possibility of coronary disease. A combination of heredity and running had shorn me of coronary risk factors. Even in early adulthood, I was marked as least likely to have a heart attack.

Adding to the security was my avoidance of the preventable causes of death. The athletic life had made me a nonsmoker and no more than a moderate drinker. My driving, while not impeccable, was guided by a defensive philosophy that kept me safe on the roads. When I took health-hazard appraisals I scored high except for one very important item—an annual checkup.

Like most Americans I had gone years and years without being examined by a physician. I recall once at an American Medical Association convention they set up a section where physicians could get a physical examination and have the routine laboratory work done. They snared hundreds in this net, many who had not been seen by a fellow doctor since their stint in the service or when taking out insurance.

Actually, what needs to be done in a physical exam requires very little time. Since there are no symptoms (or the person would have already sought help), the history takes only a few minutes. The laboratory work takes only minutes more. This leaves time so that even a ten-minute visit is adequate for a physical examination. And here we should be searched for those silent but life-threatening malignancies. When risk factors for heart disease are absent, the examination should concentrate on breast, prostate, and colon abnormalities. Any suspicious skin findings or abnormal lymph glands should be noted.

The evidence for prevention is not as clear in cancer as it is in coronary disease. With cancer our main aim is early detection. Daily I meet people long after an early cancer was detected and removed from their body. There are now medical miracles occurring with later and later detection, but nothing surpasses finding a malignancy early and dealing with it before there has been a chance for it to spread.

I know all this now. And you do, too. Being a physician I am very much aware of this need for early discovery. The education of the public has paralleled that of the medical community. Most people have learned that cancer is curable if it is caught soon enough.

However, most people take the view that it will not happen to them.

I am one of them.

Y OU ONLY LIVE ONCE," SAID THE HUMORIST FRED Allen, "but if you do it right, once is enough." The import of this aphorism undoubtedly varies with our age. In our ascendant years we know just how to go about living life successfully. At forty-five we are torn between trying to remedy the mess we have made or going back and starting over. I can attest to two truths: It is still possible to do it right, and no, I would not want to go through it again.

Life is a long, hard struggle. But it is also a positive-sum game. Everybody can win. The lives of other people, relatives, friends, public figures may serve as inspiration or

warnings but do not add or detract from our performance.

The successful life in many ways is difficult to define.
Satisfaction is internal. Establishing behavioral criteria for
success is difficult. The profiles we use frequently miss the
mark. Success in marriage, a good health record, ability to
enjoy a vacation, and doing better than one's parents may
well identify successful people. Still, many who have
failed in all those categories may feel good about doing it
their way.

Doing things right means doing things right for us. At
my age this emerges as a primary rule in life. From my
porch I look at the passing throng on the boardwalk and
note the development of character with age. The young
are homogenous, but each of the elderly stands out. They
are no longer members of the herd.

To some degree we differ from everyone else in the
world. Whatever the general rule, it has to be applied individually. We function in fundamentally different ways
in areas as diverse as religion, art, and physical activity.
Our careers are, or should be, *vocation*—a call heard only
by our own ears.

How varied we are is only too evident. Consider the
religious life, and count the different ways in which that
life can be led. If science be preferred, how many the
forms of expression. We have only to read *The Varieties of*

Religious Experience by William James and *The Varieties of Human Values* by Charles Morris to see the enormously different ways in which we find peace and happiness on one hand and virtue and strength on the other.

Fortunately, we set forth on this journey equipped for success. The powers we need are available to all. The *arete* or excellence sought by the Greeks is possible for anyone. The Sermon on the Mount is writ large on every heart. Even the bad experiences are universal and corrective. Distrust, guilt, isolation, and despair can bring us to know and practice their opposites and get us back on track.

Although good fortune may be needed for happiness, it appears that what is essential to the good life is always available. Thornton Wilder pointed this out in writing about *Our Town:* "I have tried to find a value above price for the smallest events in our daily life."

That daily life is the setting and stage for our own drama. We come to know that we fail or succeed according to how we handle the ordinary, commonplace events going on around us. It is in apparently trivial events that we most clearly show who we are. Not mortal sins but venial sins alter lives. And they reveal the lukewarm, the would-be respectable trimmers.

Allen was right. Make this one life you have a work of art. Live with class and you'll go out in style.

. . .

I N HIS LECTURE ON "THE VALUE OF SAINTLINESS,"
William James centers on the topic of asceticism.
The Greek root of this word has to do with athletic
training. And James at one point refers to athletes as "sec-
ular saints," and to saints as "athletes of God."

This follows from his belief that life should be a struggle. "Life is made," he states, "in being and creating and
suffering." People who subscribe to this opinion are "the
twice-born"; they believe that "there is an element of real
wrongness in the world, which is neither to be ignored
nor avoided."

James felt that this "element of wrongness" must be
squarely overcome by heroic action and then cleansed
away by suffering. Anyone who doesn't meet and overcome pain and wrong and death is not really inside the
game. He lacks the great *initiation*.

"In these remarks," writes James, "I am leaning only
upon mankind's common instinct for reality, which in
point of fact has always held the world to be essentially a
theatre for heroism." James goes even further on our need
to be heroic. "In heroism, we feel, life's supreme mystery
is hidden. Each of us in his own person feels that a high-
hearted indifference to life would expiate all his short-
comings."

The more one reads James the more evident it is that he does have an answer. Even if the answer is Rilke's "Live the question." For James, the way to live the question is to lead the ascetic life.

"Asceticism must, I believe, be acknowledged to go with the profounder way of handling the gift of existence." James then puts forth the same message in far fewer words: "The strenuous life tastes better." And throughout his writings is the implication that we need a moral equivalent of war. He espoused a belief which he said could be recognized by common sense, i.e., "That he who feeds on death that feeds on men possesses life supereminently and excellently, and meets best the secret demands of men."

One moral equivalent of war is facing the death-dealing final disease. Willy-nilly the dying person is given the opportunity to live the questions. The initiation, however long avoided, is about to begin. The once-born sentimental optimist now clearly sees the element of real wrongness in the world. From now on comes the awareness that life is "neither farce nor genteel comedy," but something we must sit at in mourning garments.

James was a physician who knew he had a disease (narrowing of the aortic valve in the heart) that was certainly going to limit his life. When he wrote his lecture on saintliness he had already had warnings that his time was short. These words are the best response to a question which he admits has no answer.

When he died he left a note: "There are no answers. There are no conclusions." Those of us who turn to James for help and inspiration are unwilling to accept that statement. It may well be true; but we must live and die in the spirit of James—always doing the best we can.

And now, Dad, as I stand at your desk looking into the early-evening light, I see your steel-blue eyes in the water, your spirit in the crashing waves, and my life on the horizon. I miss you. I'm scared to be without you, but I realize I can always find comfort in the memories of the days spent together. The morning coffee, conversations, and listening to "Graceland" on the stereo. "Graceland," the song that soothed the pain for both of us. The words and music telling us everything would be okay. "Poorboys and Pilgrims"—that's us, Dad.

MONICA

A Healthy Way to Be Ill

IN HIS NEW YEAR'S NOTE, A FRIEND SUGGESTED I spend my seventieth year deciding what I want to be when I grow up. He is quite right. At my age, one can no longer dodge the great questions. Why am I here? Where am I going?

I am now technically, and in various other ways, an old man. I should, by now, have had sufficient experience in the world to know that no other questions are of real importance. But I have been here for seven decades and still have not reached my philosophical puberty. I have no answers.

It's past time for me to grow up. I should have done it

years ago. How long can one remain a child? If I am an example, the answer is a very long time—even a lifetime. I could look upon this delay as an achievement—my friend does—and as Picasso once said, "It takes a long time to become young." Seeing life as a game, viewing the world as a schoolyard, remaining forever at play are states of mind perhaps more to be desired than deplored.

At my age growing up is an ominous thought. Growing up is preparing for death. The questions unanswered for a lifetime now quite obviously have to do with death and dying. Yet that does preclude making what remains of life an even more exciting game. One can, it seems, grow up and still remain a child.

"Old men ought to be explorers," writes T. S. Eliot. A capital idea. Children, as we well know, are the best explorers. The grandchildren arrive at our house and soon unearth things long lost and other treasures presumably safely secreted from their probings. Eliot, in "East Coker," reminds us that for old men, "Here and there does not matter/We must be still and still moving/Into another intensity/For a further union, a deeper communion. . . ."

Besides the aged, only the child knows this game. Adults deal with the intricacies of the unknown. They become adept at the having and the getting: the deeds and wealth of their generation. Children and old men venture beyond the known, to the terra incognita that surrounds our lives.

Once I was driving along a national seashore bordering the Gulf south of Corpus Christi. The ribbon of road was flanked by dunes as far as the eye could see and suddenly I had the thought that the earth might well be flat. I could come to the end and fall off. I had the feeling of a beginner at this marvelous game of life.

I am traveling toward another horizon that may represent either the end of everything or some transition to a new and better existence. We all are, of course. But to those of my age it is becoming quite important whether we will no longer be—or enter eternity.

A decade or so ago such considerations never entered my consciousness. It is only when age becomes evident and diminishing powers herald a major change that meditations turn to that not-too-far-off future. I was brought up confident of eternal life. My worry was not the fact of eternity, but whether it would be spent in heaven or hell. The concept of sin drives the hereafter into hiding places of the subconscious so we can direct our attention to living without guilt or shame.

But only the very young and the quite old can do that. The beauty of age is that life becomes quite simple. It gets beyond good and evil. The complexities that worry us through our adult years are seen for what they are—tortuous entanglements involving a few central themes. They are much like a catastrophic knotting of wires which, when unraveled, proves to contain only one or two strands.

The growing child and the growing seventy-year-old have many things in common, but none more evident than two great yearnings: the desire for love and the desire for knowledge. I think sometimes of myself in fifth grade—I never learned so much or felt more at home— and I know that is what I want to be again. I am here to gain knowledge and know love, and wherever I am going I know that will continue.

I'm sure my friend will not be surprised to hear that when I grow up I want to be a fifth grader.

I AM, AND WILL BE UNTIL I DIE, A SELF IN EVOLUTION. The passage of time does not bring age but maturity. I reach a stage, master it, and pass to the next. If I fail, that failure will persist until I rectify it. No amount of years will rid me of that necessity.

My self is not my body, although for most of my life I thought so; did I not have control of my body? Epictetus, who defined the self as what we could control, said no. And once disease and age set in, I recognized that truth. I can get the most out of my body. I can be an athlete. But the athlete I am and the maximum performance I can attain is my body's domain, not mine.

Nevertheless, I am my body. It is the instrument through which I experience myself and the world. With it I have immediate and exciting and illuminating communication with other people. My body is the prime mover in the evolution of this self.

My self is not my mind, either. Although for most of my life I thought so. As physician and writer I depended on my mental skills. As they diminished I saw my self diminishing with them. My self-image, this product of the body experiencing and the mind interpreting, rested on the level of each function.

Every athlete or artist is extremely aware of this problem. And just as the supremely talented are in constant competition with their previous selves, all of us are. I am no different. A gifted guitarist hits periods of depression, knowing he can't sustain his level of playing. An internationally known pianist remarks that five or six times a day he worries about failure. We do the same.

This prescinds from age but is almost always exaggerated by it. We know of artists who peaked in their thirties and slipped back into obscurity. Athletic powers decline by the forties and from then on one must settle for age-group competition. Exceptions abound, but the general rule is for the body-mind machine to decline.

What does not decline is the soul. The soul is forever young, forever growing, forever gaining new powers and new insights. True, it must use the body and the mind to gain these powers. The values and virtues forever in the process are gained through the body and the mind. Until they fail completely, my self, which is my soul, will continue to grow.

This evolution is not automatic. We must have the experiences and we must learn from those experiences. We embark at birth on a lifelong education—first under the direction of others, but soon on a voyage in which we are the captain. We determine the cargo, the route, and the destination.

What happens should not be happenstance. It is not enough to be a member of the herd. I must take charge or someone else will. Either individuals or groups will be making my self for me. I will be accepting as success what may well be failure. I will be establishing goals that are no more than way stations.

I cannot neglect the rules for my body. And I should study with Emerson the natural history of the intellect. I am not about to sacrifice anything potential—whether it be energy or creativity. And at the same time I can be enlarging my soul as well.

Let us think for a while of the virtues and strengths we need and how we can attain them. Much has been written in support of Erikson's stages of life, and of Abraham Maslow's basic human needs. The Baltimore Catechism lists the "Gifts of the Holy Ghost." These stages and needs and gifts are not determined by intelligence. We learn through common sense, faith, and experience. What we need is available to every one of us.

Each of us has a body-mind instrument, however flawed, through which we can make our soul. That is the secret of life. "This world is a vale for soul making." And the world, things, people are necessary for that soul making.

Raising one's consciousness is essential. That is the prime mental preparation. We go back to ancient injunctions and their translations in our own classics. "Live each day as if it were your last," writes Marcus Aurelius. "Every day is doomsday," echoes Emerson. "Become the thing you are," say the Greeks.

I N MY BOYHOOD YEARS IN BROOKLYN I WAS A DIE-hard Dodger fan. One manifestation of this was checking on who won the game. And if there was one rule in Brooklyn, it was, "You do not joke about ball-game scores." No excuses could be given or accepted for such loutish behavior.

When I had the first biopsy of my prostate it was reported to be normal. It was equivalent to telling me the Dodgers had beaten the Giants when they had actually lost, because it turned out that the biopsy was positive—

and I was entering the final phase of my life with death from prostate cancer.

Adjustment, as in losing the euphoria of a Dodger victory over the hated Giants, was difficult. Not only bad news, but the worst of bad news. It was not a return to a neutral state—no game at all, "not proven," lost biopsy, or other information of little psychological impact.

No. Here I was given in two minutes over the phone a new role in a new play. My unique, never-to-be-repeated event had altered course. I was to improvise from day to day, producing and writing my own drama.

TWENTIETH-CENTURY SPANISH PHILOSOPHER José Ortega y Gasset told us that we live our lives like a sleepwalker who is carried to the wings of a theater—then, awakened with a push, is thrust down to the footlights and before the public.

Then, in a situation that is not sought, prepared for, or foreseen, we must act. "So life is given to us," writes Ortega, or better yet, it is thrown at us. It is a problem we must resolve. To live, said Ortega, is continually deciding what we are going to be. We write, produce, and act out our own drama. Life is fired at us point-blank; we must constantly decide what to do with it.

So it is with my cancer. Suddenly I am a person with a

fatal disease. Accompanying it are a variety of dysfunctional states. I am no longer the athlete I was. There is a tremendous difference between being sick and being well. In dramatic terms my play has to take this change into account. My life is not ready-made. I must make it myself.

This new life is strange to me. My old lifestyle was such that if I wasn't holier than thou, I was certainly healthier than thou.

Now I look like a scarecrow. I am not the romantic lead in this play. I am nevertheless an important individual—and it is from my experience as an individual that I will discover the universal law behind it.

That is the hope we bring to all experience. We can look for meaning or, as Joseph Campbell suggests, settle for the experience itself. So my life proceeds each day. And it consists, as do all lives, of doing one thing rather than the other. Decisions are the meat of my day. I follow the instructions of William James: "Will you or won't you have it so?"

How best to handle this affliction? I must deal with restrictions I would not have believed a short time ago. I am going through the familiar stages of a play, from the Greeks to Broadway. First the exposition—the hero, me, in equilibrium with my environment. Life is free and easy. Then comes the loss of equilibrium—imposed by outside forces.

Following this comes the resolution, the dénouement. Life is either dramatic or theatrical. Molière said, "Life is a play with a badly written third act."

My story, my play is that of a life filled with the best. I was never given anything I could not handle. I believe therefore that living with cancer is within my powers.

Ortega pointed the way. He spells out the necessary qualifications for success. "Noblesse oblige" is always his theme. He is an elitist. He defines the person who goes beyond what is required. Cancer does that. It goes beyond what is required. My fellow sufferers have defined the qualities that are needed to make every day count. And like everything in our daily life, we are born equal. These virtues and values are available to us.

My cancer can provoke monologues, soliloquies, conversations, community, any number of dramatic devices. The most important thing to keep in mind is Thornton Wilder's attempt to make each day's event be of tremendous importance.

Our Town, which is filled with thoughts on death and the brevity of human existence, is the classic example of the significance of death. The characters, each in his own way, deal with death. They come back, have the revelation, and return to the shades.

Each day I do the same. I awaken early, take my medication, and then try to be productive despite my disabled body.

Rewriting the third act may prove more difficult. However, I look toward the "new me" who will eventually capitulate to the tumor—and wonder how it will end. When I take the final bow, who will I be?

WHEN I LEARNED I HAD INOPERABLE CANCER of the prostate that had spread to the bones, I went through a familiar sequence: pain, then denial, and finally depression. I lay awake nights thinking of this alien eating up my body. I stopped scheduling talks. I began to live with death.

In time I realized that this was not the end. If one is lucky, the prostate tumor is testosterone dependent. Remove the testosterone from the body, and the tumor stops growing and even regresses. In time the cells that did not need the hormone for growth will take over. But that can be far down the road. Several years perhaps. Maybe even a decade.

I was one of the lucky ones. Offered the choice of castration, female hormones, or a daily injection of hypothalamic hormone Gn-RH, I chose the last—and it worked. In fact it was almost miraculous. The pain disappeared, the bone scan improved, and serial tests of Prostatic Specific Antigen showed only a negligible amount of cancer tissue in my body. Still, I remained apprehensive. If there is one guarantee on any form of castration it is that the cancer will eventually break through. The enemy will win the war.

I also had to worry about the other life-limiting conditions that come with my age—some perhaps with more immediate consequences. "People with prostate cancer," said my son the endocrinologist, "usually die of something else." Strangely, that actually cheered me up. I remembered something Bill Bradley said about his attitude when training for basketball: "I might lose because I wasn't tall enough; I might lose because I wasn't fast enough. But I wasn't going to lose because I wasn't ready." I decided then and there, I might die of prostate cancer but I was certainly not going to die of anything else.

There is much to be said about the importance of attitude in dealing with one's cancer. It refers mostly to a state of mind. A life filled with love and laughter will get you through. That, and imagery. See your body killing off the cancer. It comes down to fighting the enemy with your mind and emotions.

This battle plan has its merits, but I like the Bradley approach. Become an athlete. Develop all the functions my body possesses. Let the cancer look for help elsewhere.

So I went about the business of making myself the best body possible. I wasn't going to die because I wasn't ready. What I could control I was determined to control.

There is good reason for people with prostate cancer to die of another disease. Their average age is sixty-seven years old. And the average sixty-seven-year-old is unfit, and carrying around risk factors for heart disease and stroke. Many, of course, have already incurred life-threatening disease. So considerable numbers succumb to heart attacks, strokes, and pulmonary disease.

Most of these fatalities can be delayed or prevented. Lifestyle at sixty-seven is even more important than in one's prime. As I age I have become determined that my physiology and metabolism approximate what they were when I was twenty-one. Nature does not bend her rules as I get older, so why should I? Allowing elders like myself to have high cholesterol, more body fat, and increments in our blood pressure makes sense only to the young doctors who take care of us. At what they consider my advanced age, health care professionals ease up on restrictions, especially for cancer patients.

"Enjoy what's left of life" is the attitude. "I prepare my patients for death," one oncologist told me. As if I would enjoy it more and be better prepared if I discarded my athletic life. Suppose I stopped running, gained fifteen pounds, drank myself into oblivion every night, and returned to smoking cigarettes. Is that the way my life should end?

I admit there is some temptation to follow the path of complete self-indulgence. But true self-indulgence is the reverse. The athletic life is the good life. Becoming the best you can be makes you feel the best you can feel. From that renewed body comes a renewed attitude that would satisfy the most ardent proponent of mind over matter.

My daily injections have not given me reprieve: my cancer has not been cured. In other instances, radiation or surgery or chemotherapy may eradicate the tumor. The person is returned to the precancerous life. I am still under sentence. I have been given, as Stewart Alsop put it, a stay of execution. Time to set things right—I was about to say, *get* things right, which is part of it, too—and achieve what I was sent here to do.

I have taken a proprietary interest in cancer. It has replaced running and its injuries in my life where there is a limited repertoire of signs and symptoms the body can manifest. Cancer, because it has a tendency to spread, presents a diverse field.

So it is with my prostate, and I almost take pleasure in doing battle. Some time ago I referred to myself as a mobile medical museum. Last year in a press interview, a TV commentator took up the same theme.

With cameras running, he asked, "What is it with you runners? You suffer stress fractures, blood in the urine, excessive asthma, plantar fasciitis. You'll run on one leg if necessary." I waited and let him run on. When he finished, I said, "It gives us bragging rights."

And so it is with cancer. Each day brings some indignity. When I awaken I am reminded by my body that I am not normal.

In that moment I feel stunned—it is different from the total reaction that will come upon later revelations. The biopsy lied once, perhaps it is lying again. I need more information that will come later. Until it does I live a provisional life.

I stood at the starting line feeling so alone and almost in tears when the starting gun exploded in my ears. The pain of the race began.

With a short uphill distance to the finish and having conceded first place to another, I was locked in a battle for second. Giving my all, I still could not break away, but as we turned the corner for home, there you stood, out of nowhere, shouting, "Now, Michael, take him on the hill."

And I did.

The emotion of that day is still indescribable, and as I told you years later, that was the day you became my father and I became your son. It had nothing to do with running—just the pure experience of letting me learn on my own, knowing that around each corner, each threshold in my life, you would be there.

MICHAEL

Running with (and Against) Cancer

J OSEPH CAMPBELL'S PRESCRIPTION FOR HAPPI-
ness was simple: "Follow your bliss." He reduced what is perhaps the most difficult task we
face to one all-encompassing command. Emerson put it just as succinctly: "Do your thing."
Implicit in both is the idea of action. Happiness
comes with effort, it is not a vicarious experience. We find
or come upon happiness through activity.

This is rarely, if ever, in the having or getting. The type
A coronary-prone individual completely occupied with
success has, according to Dr. Milton Friedman, a "spiritual sickness." He has confused the true self with the self

that consists of what he has and what people think about him. He has lost contact with his true being—and with it the happiness to which he is entitled.

Our true being consists of body, mind, and spirit, which suggests that happiness can occur in any one of these three functions of our personality. I suspect, however, that when we "Follow our bliss" or "Do our thing," whether it be at the moment physical or mental or emotional, happiness fills our entire being. Call it a "peak experience" or *satori,* such experiences fill every nook and cranny of my person.

One way I follow my bliss is by running. This is a happiness that comes directly from my body and what my body has accomplished. And concurrent with the physical bliss, my thoughts and emotions are lifted as well. Few events surpass the happiness of a locker room after winning a championship or running on a winning relay team.

Part of this is the triumph, the accomplishment, but even more is doing well at what you do best. But the running itself is primary: being for a brief moment all you can be, and the wonderful lassitude that follows all-out effort, and the fellowship. You might call it a communion of saints that is as real as the sweat and sounds that fill the room.

As we age we stop following our physical bliss. The body is pampered rather than challenged. It is told to be quiet, and becomes no more than a receptacle for the mind and spirit. Life becomes a matter of creature comforts. The challenge becomes its ability to withstand the effects of our bad habits. We are no longer athletes. We have become spectators.

This will never do. Among Emerson's instructions for the good life was another terse statement: "Be first a good animal." Life is not a spectator sport. Only to the good animal come the peak experiences, the joys, the epiphanies. All of us are Olympians. And each day brings with it success or failure that is visible, as it were, only to ourselves. How this plays out is determined much more by our body than we think. "The body is the source of energy," said Plato. We are our bodies, our bodies are us, and we must live this life physically and at the top of our powers.

My happiness has little to do with attaining goals. Emily Dickinson said it well: "Success is counted sweetest/By those who ne'er succeed." Still there are some, like Mortimer Adler, who argue that only death and its final scorecard can determine whether we were happy. And it is one of the prayers of the Church that a person have the grace of a happy death.

My experience is that when happiness occurs it is short-lived. It is a very transitory state. I may go through long periods of comfort and contentment but I do not equate them with the wholeness and holiness that comes with happiness.

I am not adept at happiness. I cannot produce it on demand, but by following the advice of Emerson, Campbell, and others I can put myself in situations where happiness is more likely to occur. What strikes me is how easy this is for children and how outrageously difficult it is for adults. This childlike capacity seems to return as one ages. If you would be happy, look at the old and the young.

"Man is an animal," writes Bertrand Russell, "and his happiness depends on his physiology more than he likes to think." Health comes first. Of course, we look to a basal state free of disease—or, at the least, free of disease limiting our daily activities.

Happiness, however, connotes more than this neutral status. Russell thought that the trained body was important. "Unhappy businessmen," he states, "would increase their happiness more by walking six miles every day than by any conceivable change in philosophy."

Walking six miles a day is quite likely to change one's philosophy as well. Thousands of walkers—and runners, swimmers, and cyclists—will attest to a new sense of life's meaning arrived at during their physical activity. The mind is in motion as well as the body.

Russell thought it was impossible to be happy without physical activity—of both mind and body. But such activity, he suggested, should be agreeable, directed to a desired end, and not contrary to our impulses.

"A dog will pursue rabbits to the point of complete exhaustion and be happy all the time, but if you put a dog on a treadmill he would not be happy because he is not engaged in a natural activity."

I am an observer of happy dogs. Daily I see numbers of them walking with their owners on the boardwalk and grass in front of our beach house. They are a curious lot, constantly in motion and exploring the world around them. At times they are engaged in play, chasing thrown sticks or pursuing Frisbees. One characteristic is immediately evident. They are very serious when having fun. They may wag their tails but they are totally concentrated on what is about to happen.

Play is of equal importance to us. The things we do with our bodies should be done merely because they are fun—not because they serve some serious purpose. If we are not doing something that is enjoyable on its own account we should look for something that is. We may not find something as natural to us as hunting is to a dog, but we can come quite close.

"When things are bad," observes Russell, "what a person needs is not a new philosophy but a new regimen—a different diet, or more exercise, or what not." That advice seems simplistic, but it worked for me. I took to the roads in my forty-fifth year and shored up a life that was coming apart.

Regimen was also the key to the Greeks' pursuit of happiness. They believed self-mastery included the mastery of the body. Their education treated the body as equal to the mind and spirit. The ancient Greeks spent time every day in the gymnasium and palestra engaged in athletic activity.

The key is movement—and movement that is play. What we do with our bodies and minds must be an end in itself as well as a means to an end. Man is an animal, as Russell states. Man is also a child, and his happiness depends more on that psychology than we suspect.

Our needs are complex. Our goals come from our highest yearnings but we must recognize our animal instincts and our childhood impulses. Integrating animal, child, and adult is a formidable task. Yet our happiness depends upon it.

What marks happy people, according to Russell, are two qualities: a stable framework built around a central purpose; and play. Our leisure should include physical play of some sort. This need not be sport, although that is the best way to guarantee play. The game, the contest, the race, the competition are not essential. What is required is the spontaneous expression of the self as body.

Happiness is a large subject, but Russell's suggestion

makes for a good start. Like Emerson and Spencer before him, he is saying if you wish to be a success in this life you must first be a good animal.

We can do that through exercise, which is boring, tedious, and repetitious. The better way is through play, which is exercise done without realizing it. The secret of the successful six-mile walk is leaving work and family, care and responsibilities behind—and entering a world that is strangely yet satisfyingly all your own.

A FEW YEARS AGO WHEN I WAS IN BOSTON FOR THE Boston Marathon I saw an advertisement in the *Globe:* "RUNNERS WANTED!" The Dana Farber Cancer Institute was recruiting runners to join them in their research activities.

"We are engaged," the ad went on, "in our own difficult kind of marathon, a long road to discover solutions to complex problems about the cause and cure of cancer." And who better to enroll than those who had become marathoners themselves? "We need people like you, people with dedication, discipline, energy and the belief you can change things for the better."

Those qualities come with the athletic experience. Whatever the sport, it develops not only the body but the mind and spirit as well. Sport is an essential element in education, a fact realized centuries ago by the Greeks, and now becoming apparent to those who, long after graduation, have returned to the task of becoming athletes.

The athletic experience consists of three parts. The training, which the Greeks called *askesis*. The event, or the Greeks' *agon*. And the aftermath, which the Greeks termed *arete* and which can be variously translated as excellence or vigor or virtue. The goal of Greek education was to produce the citizen-soldier. This education, said Plato, was what trains one from childhood in virtue, and makes one able to rule the state or defend it.

The aim is self-mastery. If we are to dominate events we must first dominate ourselves. Self-rule comes naturally to the athlete. Training, or *askesis,* brings with it the virtues of prudence and moderation. The lifestyle of athletes conforms to the laws of the body. Breaking training is physical sin. When I became a runner, I became my body and accepted its laws. This does not, of course, go unrewarded. Athletes perform at the peak of their powers.

But self-mastery goes beyond the preparation. The race becomes the *agon* where the self is developed. "The race to be run, the victory to be won, the defeat that one risked suffering," writes Michel Foucault about the Greeks, "these are processes and events that took place between oneself and oneself. The adversaries the individual had to combat were not just with him and close by—they were part of him."

How well the runner knows this. At first it appeared that I was fighting hills and terrain, heat and humidity and the distance I had to race. But it was soon apparent that these were not my opponents. My opponent is me. The real me who would let this cup pass. The true self who is willing to settle for "a good try," and not the last desperate and painful and revealing plunge into the black hole of who I am.

The importance of sport has not been lost on philosophers. George Santayana wrote, "There is then a great and continuous endeavor, a representation of all the primitive virtues and fundamental gifts of man." In the race the runner searches for these virtues and values, the martial values now liberated from the attendant horrors of war. We have then, as Santayana states, "A drama in which all moral and emotional interests are involved. The whole soul is stirred by a spectacle that represents the basis for life."

Is this an exaggeration? Robert Frost, attending an All-Star game, joined athletes and rejoiced in their display of prowess, courage, knowledge, and justice. We see again and again the elevation of the whole person. Educators forced to reevaluate the athletic experience come to the same conclusions. A faculty committee at Dickinson College, considering the role of sports in the student's life, writes, "The agon is not a matter of winning or losing. It is the willingness to compete—let us not forget that the agon is freely accepted—it is a matter of committing the self to act and bear the consequences of action."

And there are other rewards seen by these educators: "To experience sport and analyze it critically is to be involved in an enterprise with dramatic and intense personal immediacy rarely, if ever, offered by more traditional studies." And the report goes on: "Sport is an easily acceptable laboratory of dedication, sacrifice, courage, mastery, order, cooperation, leadership, companionship, solitude, loyalty, authority, etc."

Therein lies the final part of the athletic experience: the transformation of the self brought about by these learning experiences. The deposition into the subconscious of the good news about the self—an entrée into a Blakean world where we become "Chariots of fire" and for which the best word is *exultation*. We are now what we became in the race and are ready for whatever the day brings.

What the day brings, as everyone learns sooner or later, is recurrent challenge. The *agon* is daily. Epictetus told us that almost two millenia ago. "If anything laborious or pleasant, glorious or inglorious be presented to you, remember now is the contest, now are the Olympic Games and they cannot be deferred."

There never will be a day when we won't need dedication, discipline, energy, and the feeling that we can change things for the better.

The people at the Dana Farber Institute know that. We should too.

ONE OF THE INTERESTS OF THE BALL STATE University Human Performance Laboratory is the physical capabilities of aging athletes. Their search for elderly specimens to study led to my receiving a phone call from Dr. David Costill, a longtime friend who is the director of the lab.

"A day and a half will do it," he said. And since athletes, even aging ones, love to be tested, I went.

Things began badly. Two simple measurements—height and weight. One of my major goals is to keep them constant. "Nature doesn't change the rules because you're seventy," I tell my audience. "I try to keep all my statistics the same as they were when I was twenty years old running cross-country at Manhattan College."

Somehow I had shrunk 2 inches and gained 18 pounds. I was no longer 5 feet 9½ inches and 136 pounds. I laid it to the treatment for my prostate cancer. The hormone deprivation must be fattening me up and giving me curvature of the spine. "Not so," said Costill, "you're eating too much, not running enough, and you should be lifting weights."

While I mulled that over, I was taken to test my lung function. First a deep inhalation, then a rapid exhalation. Following that was a prolonged period of breathing as deep and as fast as I could. I felt completely inadequate gasping to a halt before my allotted time was up. Then I was told I had achieved 127 percent of my predicted result. The physiologists apparently do not expect much from a seventy-year-old.

There were more insults to me. Next I was strapped into a Cybex machine and encouraged to extend my leg as quickly and as energetically as possible; and then to just as quickly flex it at the knee. The object of this game was to measure the strength of my quadriceps (the front thigh muscles) and my hamstrings (the back thigh muscles).

Dr. Dale Pearson, the strength expert in this fitness cabal, was my coach. He kept encouraging me to try harder and harder. Beside me was a computer screen providing graphic evidence of my effort. By now I was in a to-the-death struggle with this device and barely registering on the screen. Despite this evidence of ineptitude, Pearson was marveling at what I was accomplishing.

Next came the bench press. I was started with a weight that a fifth-grade student could have lifted with one arm. As I progressed 10 pounds at a time, Pearson was becoming lyrical about my performance. Then at 95 pounds I came to a dead stop. This had little impression on Pearson's evaluation. He went to tell the staff how great I was. I was beginning to wonder if their previous seventy-year-olds were terminally ill when they were tested.

More bad news was to come. The dreaded stress test, the all-out effort to determine my maximum oxygen uptake, was next. I began at a ten-minute-mile pace and was uncomfortable for the first six minutes. Then, as the speed was increased, my right hamstring, stressed by the Cybex, went into spasm.

I continued despite the pain, using all the sore-hamstring tricks I knew, and got my speed up to eight-and-a-half-minute miles. But ten minutes into the test I capitulated to the run. I signaled them to stop.

Once again the examining team was delighted. My uptake was 33 ml/kg/min. About as good as an average seventy-year-old should be. Since this had dropped considerably from the 56 I had registered a decade ago, I was upset. But the more depressing the results were to me, the more elated the lab became.

There was a lot more to come. A biopsy of my calf muscle, bone scans to see if my bones were getting thin (the non-weight-bearing ones were; others were getting thicker). Then a CAT scan to check out the fat on my legs and on my arms. The resulting films showed very little fat on my legs, a good deal more on my arms. I knew where most of it was—on my midriff. I had gone from a thirty-one-inch waist to a thirty-three.

The next morning I had blood drawn and learned that I had little hope of dying of heart disease. My cholesterol was 155 and HDL was 50—world-class values.

My final stop was a sports medicine clinic where I had an examination for muscle and joint problems. Beyond those common to most runners—tight hamstrings—I had none. My knee X rays were free from arthritis.

On the plane back from Muncie I remembered the words of Dr. Michael Pollack, who has also studied seventy-year-old athletes. The trouble with seventy-year-olds, said Pollack, is they don't train enough.

I'll drink to that. There was nothing Costill and his crew found that I couldn't improve if I worked hard enough. I simply have to take dead aim at the collegian I was in 1940 and get back to that future.

B ACK AT HOME ON THE JERSEY SHORE, I WENT for a forty-minute run with my daughter. The next day I joined a dozen or more runners for the Saturday morning run—a fixture in our town for the past fifteen years. This was followed by breakfast at a pancake place and an hour of laughter before we broke up and headed for home.

I mention these runs because they are completely out of character with the runner I once was. For me running was two experiences: solitary training runs and all-out competition. If I was not antisocial, I was asocial. I went to a place, waited for my award, and went home.

Cancer has its rewards, and one of them has been finding other values in my running. My therapy has put me far back in the race. When I come to the finish line there are few runners behind me. Competition, and the trophies that go with it, no longer attracts me. For the first time the most important thing about running has become my fellow runners.

When I run now I am a nonstop talker. It is as if I spent the last six months in Antarctica alone, like Admiral Byrd—and I can't wait to find out what's going on in the rest of the world. And this is not a monologue, but a conversation.

A T ONE OF OUR POSTRACE PARTIES, ONE RUNNER had to leave early. In the past few years he had been faced with caring for his sick parents.

Our current medical care has been able to postpone dying. Americans are living longer than ever. What it has not done is prolong successful living. As we near our last years we are now threatened with the prospect of being one of the living dead.

If I polled the fifty or more runners chatting out on the deck or inside watching the Olympics on why they ran, I would get a variety of answers. People run for physical, mental, psychological, and social reasons. But almost universally they plan to run for the rest of their lives. It is that sentiment that interested Wilfred Graham, a professor of religion at Michigan State University. In questioning twenty women runners he found this secondary but universal motivation expressed in one way or another: "I'm going to run until I can't put one foot in front of another and then I'll be dead. No geriatrics ward for me."

"Running is a scientifically approved way of extending life," writes Graham. "Runners, however, do not so much want to gain an extension as they want to insure mobility until death comes." Runners' seeming preoccupation with youth and their defiance of age is actually their dread of what Graham calls *terminal helplessness*.

That, it seems, is the deeper meaning of "I'll run until I drop." Death, as it does for every age, will come to the runner. It is beyond our control. What is possible, however, is what is technically called "compression of morbidity." This means limiting the disability and dependence of our final years to a minimum. The ideal would be to emulate the wonderful one-horse shay that lasted for a hundred years and dissolved into dust in a single instant.

Graham firmly believes that many converts to running have done so to guarantee that their bodies will not slowly decay in a convalescent home. "Hidden somewhere in the pursuit of regular exercise is the notion that if one keeps moving, one will never be caught in the wires and tubes and sterile unprivacy that the aged suffer today."

I heard one story of a man in his late sixties whose family decided to put him in a nursing home. When he heard that he said, "I came to the realization that my lifestyle must be completely wrong." He completely reversed his way of living, followed nature's rules, and remained independent.

A nursing home is probably not in the consciousness of my partying runner friends who have just finished a five-mile race. Nevertheless, a little probing can bring it to light. After all, many if not most of these runners began running in their mid-thirties, a time when the body provides subtle but definite clues that you are on the downslope of life. With a life expectancy of seventy-two, thirty-six becomes middle age and instinctively people know it.

My own aim is to live out the biblical span and more, with as little "down time" as possible—to be a competitor in life, right up to my final days. The athletic life protects me as long as possible. I dread to join the thousands who, as Graham points out, "languish in homes for the aged, their minds and spirits exhausted but their bodies helpless to die."

I looked around at the lean, fit, vital people of all ages who filled our house, and remembered my thoughts jogging to the starting line earlier that day. "This is a great day to run. This is a good day to die."

P LAY IS ESSENTIAL TO THE GOOD LIFE. WE NEED IT to become fully functioning human beings. Play brings with it three forces that are necessary for our development and for the life we wish to lead.

Often we do not recognize the lack of play in our lives. We are unaware of the effects it would have on all the functions of our personality. We live without the forces available to us in every aspect of our being. We operate without this force which would transform our day-to-day living.

The first influence of play is on our bodies. It brings with it exercise. Medicine and surgery attack disease but they do not cover health. That resides in the fully functioning body, be it sick or well. Health is the best we can be. Health is getting the most out of the body we were born with. The playful use of the exercising body is what brings this about.

The second influence of play is on our attitude. It encourages a sense of humor. The normal individual, said

Freud, must be able to work and love. Before either comes play. You can approach a project with deadly seriousness or you can come to it laughing as if it were of little moment. Humor combines both. It allows us to be serious while having the feeling that it is all a game. Or we can come to a project knowing it is a game yet realizing how serious that game is. Frost looked at this and said it plain: "Work becomes play for mortal stakes."

The final effect of play is on our conduct. The third force introduced by play is experience. Either tradition or logic may hold sway, but we must make our own truth. We must learn from ourselves. We must trust the inner person. The experiences in play are immediate, graphic, and illuminating. We learn the fundamental characteristics of our own personal human nature. In play we reveal ourselves—to others as well as to ourselves. Play is an unrivaled area for self-discovery.

Play makes each one of us an athlete. Training becomes a way of life—which is for the best, since it is essential. No less for us than for the Greeks is the *agon,* the contest part of our life. And no less than for the Greeks is it necessary to train to be an athlete to meet it.

"Play," declares Joan Cass in *Helping Children Grow Through Play,* "is as necessary and important to a child as the food he eats, for it is the very breath of life to him, the reason for his existence and his assurance of immortality."

Now in my second childhood, I can assure you it is as true when you are seventy as it was when you were seven. Play is as essential to the aged as it is to the young. I count that day lost when I am not moved to tears or laughter, but even more if I have not played.

Cass is, of course, writing of play in all its aspects. She includes invention and make-believe, the use of the imagination and acting out self-created dramas. This play-acting is a necessity, she says, because "Children unaccustomed to freedom, independence and making decisions for themselves can be bewildered, frightened and stampeded into foolish behavior when suddenly faced with situations that are new and unexpected."

Children can learn to live real life through the world of play. This is a world where defeat and despair, ignominy and disgrace last no longer than it takes to get home for supper. It is a land of knowledge and wisdom whose only price is having fun. It is a country where every citizen begins each day fresh, free of any consequences of the day before.

Not that play is easy. It demands every ounce of a child's energy. But what rewards! Psychiatrist John Bowlby is quoted by Cass: "It develops skills of both body and mind. How to compete, how to take hard knocks, how to win gracefully. Play offers healing for hurts and sadness. It breaks down tension and releases pent-up urges toward self-esteem."

It is quite easy to see that play and its effects are essential whatever one's age, but its necessity and importance become more evident in the last stage of life. When we are young we sense that life is a game. When we become old we see it as a fact.

Not all of us, of course, and in any case not immediately. It is a learning process. "Man comes to each age of his life a novice," writes French aphorist Sébastian-Roch Nicholas Chamfort. Philosophers would have us believe differently. We grow in various ways. Hit a zenith and then gradually decline. Whatever our age, we are the same person gradually bringing our talents to a peak and then fading away.

But now at seventy living with cancer, I find I am a novice. I have to begin at the beginning. And much like a child I have to make play the center of my life, and through it learn how to live in this new age. Now I need everything my previous years taught me—and more. I am like a fresh new intern just graduated from medical school and now required to act on my own. Free, independent, and forced to make decisions.

But now life is the game, not medicine. And time is running out. Now is the time to play with intensity, to experience myself in challenging situations, using all my energy.

JUST BEFORE MY HORMONE THERAPY BEGAN TO FAIL, and the cancer went on the move, I ran a race close to home.

When I neared the two-mile mark of the five-mile race in Ocean County Park, there was a park ranger keeping us on course. I was dead last, 107th in a field of 107 runners.

As I passed, he called out to me, "How are you doing?"

"The best I can," I answered.

Doing the best I can is no more than routine, but being last was an unusual experience.

Early on, when I returned to running in my forties, I ran in a national cross-country championship. I was lapped by the entire field, but never since then had I held the position that defines the end of race. There was no question this time that I was last. I turned around several times to be certain. I was surrounded by silence, as if I were alone on a training run in those woods.

Then came final proof. I could hear just behind me the vehicle that brings up the rear. Most races have one to pick up those who, for one reason or another, injury or exhaustion, might need help getting back to the finish line.

About two hundred yards ahead was my friend Jason, holding his steady pace, and beyond him at some distance a small group of stragglers that I could see intermittently through the trees. Each of us was engaged in a private struggle, trying to maintain the level of exertion a five-mile race demands—between hard and very hard.

This was a two-loop course, and as I neared the halfway point there was a brief time when I was tempted to drop out. This was not something new to me. On loop courses where there is an opportunity every lap to pack it in, I often have a transient impulse to call it quits.

But just as in wartime there are cowards but no cowardice, in races there are quitters but no one ever quits. Within a few strides the thought passed, and I knew if I started into the second loop it would never come again.

It never did. I was last and probably would finish last, but it didn't matter. If you asked me why I continued to race I would be unable to put it into words—nor would, I suspect, any runner, coach, or sports psychologist.

If anyone has been able to, it is the philosopher William Barrett in *The Illusion of Technique*. Barrett writes of the runner lapped by the entire field, torturing himself to keep going, as "more admirable than the victor we crown." And of the last-place finisher in the Boston Marathon he writes, "There simply cannot be a question of his quitting. An image of a man of faith."

My father's influence and intelligence are still embodied in my every decision. "If you don't have problems, you are not living," he would say. His warmth and fragility were unparalleled. His legs were all but gone, legs that had carried him through all the miles, the success, the beauty, and the magnificence of his life. One night, as I helped him up the stairs, each step was a challenge, the grunts and groans expelling the pain and weakness in his body, almost signifying life itself. The challenge Dad has left me is to respond to those steps with the strength of the athlete, the intellect of the scholar, and the determination of a man.

STEPHEN

The Physician and the Patient

HEN I STOPPED SEEING patients a number of years ago to devote my time to writing and speaking, my mother thought I had retired. "Your father would never have retired," she told me. It was useless to tell her I hadn't retired. She had been a doctor's wife. She knew I was no longer doing what doctors did. I was only two years older than my father was when he died—and I was deserting the profession. That was the way she saw it.

And the way she saw it was the way it was. When I was young no one in my profession retired. The doctor died in harness. Only a terminal illness would keep a physician from the practice that began upon graduation and continued until the eulogy at the funeral.

Others aimed for retirement. White-collar worker or blue-collar worker, they counted the years until their release. But not those in medical practice. Their work was everything. They were what they did.

Now ten years away from my office and the emergency room and the coronary care unit, I'm beginning to think my mother was right. I am retired. What I am is not what I was. I have scratched my name from the list. I refuse to do what I spent a lifetime learning to do well.

"Dr. Sheehan," my former secretary told me the other day, "you were the best." Maybe so, but I don't remember it that way. I know that my best was never enough for me. Hardly a day went by that I did not meet defeat, know failure, and feel guilt. "Life is fired at you point-blank," writes Ortega. The doctor in practice is constantly in this situation. The diagnosis must be made and the treatment instituted without the luxury of scientific certainty. I felt as if I were spending my life out on a tightrope.

So it was easy when the demand for lectures escalated and I was forced to make a choice. I closed down my practice. I became a full-time advocate of health and fitness. I now avoid the title of *Doctor*. I introduce myself simply as George Sheehan, no longer a doctor.

And in truth I am not. Ten years away from medicine is a century. If I were to practice now I would have to follow the example of a great general practitioner I once knew. This man loved his patients and shepherded them through life. If he had a specialty it was people—and he saw to it that they got the best care. "When they get sick," he once told me, "I send them to a doctor."

There have been drawbacks to my new life. When the writing goes poorly, I miss the satisfaction and excitement of dealing with emergencies and the critically ill. But I've enjoyed not being on call every other night and every other weekend, which had been my life for thirty-five years. I've liked being my own boss instead of having hundreds who could demand my presence anytime they felt it necessary.

What I've missed most is what makes medicine such a rewarding profession. Only the clergy have a goal higher than that of physicians. For all the down periods, medicine provides moments of joy and satisfaction that are difficult to find elsewhere. I remember once when a nurse asked me when I was going to take a vacation. I looked at her in surprise and then asked, "Why in the world would I want to take a vacation?"

Nevertheless, I did take a vacation, then a sabbatical, and finally, let me admit it, I retired. Retired from medicine, but not from life. It was possible, as I did, to stop what I did for a living and indeed be in a position where I didn't need to do anything for a living. But I still had to give my life meaning. I had to create reasons for living. So I have replaced my patients with listeners and readers.

In truth, my mother and I to the contrary, I am still a doctor, trying to teach people how to live the good life.

The loss of patient contact has made this difficult. My medical practice gave me what Henry James said came with living in Manhattan: "Accessibility to experience." Every patient was a novel should I care to read it. Every patient, a learning experience, a source of stories for columns or talks.

This is what I've missed. Not the intellectual delight that comes from solving problems but the sudden revelation, the illuminating remark and absolutely perfect description that can make every encounter between doctor and patient a source of wisdom and grace.

Maybe I will find it again as a patient.

YEARS BACK DOCTORS RARELY TOLD THE TRUTH. I know that I didn't. There were many reasons for this. Only one seemed legitimate—to conceal from the patient that his or her illness was cancer.

Explaining disease to a patient can be quite difficult. My father, a physician, would dispose of it by saying, "It's part of your condition." The Irish family at home, when informed of my father's judgment, was usually satisfied.

Other aspects, diet and exercise and overall lifestyle, did not require any prevarication. Errors were obvious to both patient and doctor. With male patients certain questions pertaining to sex were never asked. With women each visit was punctuated with sympathetic advice—and this too was sufficient.

Cancer, however, was different. For some reason all agreed (and at times the patient as well, by not asking any questions) that the diagnosis of cancer should be concealed. As a fledgling physician I started using code words—*mitosis* (splitting of normal cells) and other words were used at the bedside when the patients were seen by the visiting professors.

I do not let this whole procedure go unchallenged. There is an art to medicine. There is a particular art to handling the cancer patient. In this dance of death many patients have given up on a cure. They don't care what they have. They dance in a silent world in a relationship with the healer that may be unequaled.

In such a situation, the cancer does not deserve to be named. Doing so brings up another philosophical question. Naming a thing is *knowing* it—possessing it. Or the reverse is knowing and possessing the patient.

Hence even those who find this unacceptable tend to use the generic. The thing is a cancer. The structure it involves should be nameless and allow the patient and physician to do their little dance of death.

It is odd also that this dance has to be done sitting down. Doctors come, look at the patient, then depart. My procedure was to come in, take a chair, start a conversation. At times, nurses who thought I was a visitor would come in to throw me out. Looking back I think I could have gone either way—concealed the cancer or told the truth about it.

It was not always easy. I was too inexperienced to realize the primacy of relief of pain. If I had to lie to a patient, he or she should at least be kept more comfortable while thinking it over.

The current picture reflects all these changes: pain relief, complete knowledge of the disease and options, free choice of available therapies, expert care from specialists in hospice procedure, freedoms that involve living wills and concepts unknown to my generation.

In my own case, I was told early on and knew to an extent the possibilities. And then grew up in a whole new era of prostate cancer. Some things never change. The afternoon and evening pain, the fatigue, the loss of appetite. And the uneasiness about what cards I had drawn.

By that I mean either a slow-growing tumor or a wildly aggressive one. A friend of mine who a short time ago was the U.S. champion walker in his age group died in six months. Another, equally athletic, in two years.

There is little reason to conceal anything from the patient. There is a strong case for truth in mending.

T HE OCCASION WAS A PUBLIC DISCUSSION OF prostate cancer. The audience was mostly men, but many came with their spouses, who were concerned with the details of diagnosis and therapy for this disease.

I was one of the four physicians on the panel. The others were a urologist and two oncologists. I was there because I had prostate cancer. I was a presenter, not because I was a physician, but because I was a *patient.*

Patients with prostatic cancer tend to be critical of physicians. Men with this type of malignancy often get conflicting advice from different doctors. They are uncertain as to whether surgery or radiation or some hormonal manipulation is best in their case.

The three specialists who preceded me acknowledged these uncertainties. There is a saying about prostatic cancer: "If it is possible to treat prostate cancer, it is necessary; if it is necessary to treat it, it is possible." Often it seems as if the *biology* of the tumor (one slow-growing, another a prairie fire), not the treatment, is decisive.

Nevertheless, extensive studies of large numbers of patients have given support to specific therapies at specific stages of the disease. Each treatment can be analyzed according to these accumulated statistics: chance of success, side effects, and long-range problems.

The physicians pointed out that the choices they recommended were based in large part on these statistics— but had to be tailored to the individual. In any case they could not guarantee that any choice would afford a cure.

When I spoke I told the audience that while asking our physicians for more than they could deliver, we should not fail in our *responsibility* as patients.

The three presentations before mine had shown how much study and time these physicians had given to making the best possible decisions to detect and treat this disease. We patients had to make our own contribution to the success of whichever program we followed.

There is a saying that people with prostate cancer usually die of something else. The implication is that the usual sixty- to seventy-year-old American male is unhealthy, unfit, and unhappy. All of which put him at risk of unnecessary disease and premature death.

Studies have shown that coronary risk factors become *more* important after sixty years of age than before. Exercise, weight loss, lowering of cholesterol, smoking cessation, and attention to hypertension become increasingly necessary. The patient's responsibility is to follow a lifestyle that will add hours to his day, and years to his life. To follow a program that gives meaning and purpose to his final years no matter how many they may be.

"Let the physicians bear the responsibility for treating your disease," I told the audience. "You must focus on a diet–exercise–stress management regimen that will restore your general health and fitness." In that way you will maximize your mental and social and spiritual life, for all the days you have left.

Remember the war cry of the cancer community: "Make every day count."

That's up to us, not our physicians.

I WAS BEING INTERVIEWED ON A TELEVISION PROGRAM about aging. The questioner, in his early fifties, asked me, "How does one become wise?" Because I am seventysomething people assume I have reached the state of wisdom. The experiences of such a long life, they believe, must have led to an enhanced ability to make the correct decisions.

I remembered then something T. S. Eliot had written:

"Where is the wisdom we have lost in knowledge?/Where is the knowledge we have lost in information?" There is the problem of wisdom in a nutshell. Two lines from a poet is better than a doctoral dissertation.

Wisdom is a product of a process. This process begins with information, proceeds through knowledge, and through what a less gifted poet, Edgar Guest, called "a heap of living," ends in wisdom.

The medical life demonstrates quite clearly these three stages. The physician, who of necessity is a perennial student, must take in an enormous amount of information. At times I feel like a data bank. I go weekly to the hospital library where I have access to 250 weekly and monthly medical journals. There is also a monthly *Index Medicus,* which contains the subjects and authors in another 3,500 publications.

Data like this come to dominate the doctor's life. Unsolicited journals flood the office mail. Meetings abound, and a certain number have to be attended each year. This is our continuing education. Essentially, however, it is no more than information and only the first stage on the road to wisdom.

Knowledge comes next. How to translate all this research, all these studies and reports, into something of use. Knowledge is taking information and putting it to use. When I was young in my medical career this proved difficult. When I was a medical student I found it almost impossible. I had not yet put in enough hours in the office and on the wards to know what information was important and what wasn't.

Derek Bok, in his critique of Harvard Medical School, pointed to the inability to handle this torrent of scientific material as one of its key failures in education. Unfortunately, such a failure is inevitable. Only experience can enable the physician to select the information needed to recognize and treat disease easily.

This ability comes with time. The patient's symptoms and signs can generate an enormous amount of reading material. Run a computer search on any laboratory test and numerous possibilities result. There is an old saying on ward rounds: "When you hear hoofbeats, don't think of zebras." Practicing doctors must be practical. Most unusual diseases are the usual diseases looking like unusual diseases. Yet the medical library is filled with discussions and reports on the medical equivalents of zebras. These accounts fascinate the student in me but are of no interest for my practice.

Wisdom is the step beyond knowledge. This is never automatic. There are many good doctors but not so many wise ones. Wisdom comes with the knowledge that the physician's purpose is to teach the good life. This implies two things—having a concept of the good life, and understanding how to live it.

Wisdom is making correct choices. Ortega said that life consists of doing one thing or the other. We must constantly choose. "Will you or won't you have it so?" asks William James. We consult wise men when we are in difficulty because we do not trust the guidance within. Information is inadequate. Knowledge is not enough. Both have to be submitted to a higher authority. Wisdom deals with the universals. The rules, if you would, for human beings.

Wisdom, when it comes, usually arrives late in life. I've known some people who were wise in their early thirties and others who died old without a clue. Most philosophers were of the mind that a person should be at least forty years of age to have enough learning experiences. Now it seems that it is much too young. The step from knowledge to wisdom is the longest one in a person's life.

S INCE I WENT PUBLIC WITH MY PROSTATE CANCER I have received numerous phone calls and letters from men with the same problem.

I have difficulty giving them specific advice. The treatment of prostate cancer is in a tremendous state of flux.

Most callers have early-stage disease with many options. I have end-stage, with very few.

Patients are bewildered by the various differing opinions they receive from physicians, who are equally unsettled by their reading of the medical literature.

"What to do and when to do it?" is the question every patient asks. Yet frequently a patient leaves the consulting room unconvinced about the course to take.

One reason for this is the number of specialties involved in treatment. Surgeons, radiotherapists, and endocrinologists all have different therapies to offer. And some endocrinologists think their therapy should precede whatever other approach is decided upon.

Another confounding factor is the matter of philosophy. Basically physicians can be divided into the "waiters" and the "treaters." The waiters believe that the biology of the tumor is more important than treatment. At seventy years of age as many as 40 percent of men have a type of low-grade prostate cancer. The waiters argue that localized cancer needs no initial treatment. It may indeed progress, but it does so slowly and can be controlled by some method of castration, either actual or by chemical means. This sort of tumor rarely causes cancer death. Some studies have followed patients for as long as ten years without any treatment.

The other group is the treaters. These physicians take the orthodox view of cancer treatment: early detection and eradication by surgery or radiation. They point to prolonged survival when these aggressive treatments are used. In selecting a therapy for the long term, statistics show little difference between these two aggressive methods. Side effects and the possibility of complications usually enter into a patient's choice.

Surgery, of course, with its possibility of complete extirpation of the tumor, is intellectually and psychologically preferable. Further, if preceded by endocrine therapy, the ease of such surgery is enhanced.

As for radiation, innovations in technique have been reported to improve its targeting ability. Yet both physician and patient suspect that some tumor tissue may escape the high-voltage therapy.

Behind this aggressive therapy is the nagging thought that it may be effective because it wasn't necessary. The successes were tumors that would not have spread to the bones and other organs anyway. And the failures were those aggressive tumors that had already, in ways undetectable in tests, seeded out into the body. In any case, somewhat less than 50 percent of patients with apparently localized cancer are cured.

Those who listen to the arguments of both sides are

likely to find themselves repeating the question asked by urologist Dr. Willet Whitmore, Jr.: "When treatment is possible, is it necessary, and when treatment is necessary, is it possible?"

Pretreatment bone scans and CAT scans and Prostate Specific Antigen determinations can aid in answering that question. Studies of biopsy material can also be helpful. A Gleason Index from one to ten tells a lot about a tumor. If it is three or less the patients should do well no matter what is done. Ploidy analysis of DNA in the cancer cell is another prognostic tool. Emploidy or normal DNA is compatible with a long life. Dysploidy, abnormal DNA, is an unsettling finding.

The unsettling findings in my tests led me to review my day. Was I able to fill it with eight hours of solid sleep and sixteen hours of happy, healthy, productive activity? Yes, but only if I maintained my diet-exercise program along with my mental gymnastics and network of family and friends. If I followed this regimen, my prostate cancer did not alter my living each day to the maximum.

The question was my life span. How many of these days do I have left? The tumor knows, I don't. What I do know is that I am determined not to die of anything else.

. . .

MY DECISION ON HOW TO LEAD MY LIFE UN-
doubtedly has had an effect on how I will
die. Pursuing a life at low risk for heart disease must, perforce, increase the risk of death from cancer, although I may live longer before I come to that
event.

That decision was mine. There is, however, another
factor to be considered. A decision already made at birth.
I was born with the temperament that predisposed me toward death from causes other than heart disease.

An ongoing study of 1,300 former Johns Hopkins
Medical School students graduating in the years 1945
through 1964, called the "Precursor Study," has shown
an association of certain temperaments—defined as a dis-
positional tendency, a given at birth—for certain diseases.

The Hopkins study theorizes that the temperamental
differences exist in the most primitive areas of the brain.
The basic differences come down to the aggressive-
confrontational attitude versus a withdrawn-passive point
of view. Experts in the field at times invite fighting this
vulnerability. They view it as a struggle between the cancer and the aggressive resistance inherent in my own cells.

The researchers have found the type of temperament
remarkably accurate in predicting what disease will develop. They conclude, "The temperament is a variable

that has predictive potential of the future health status of the individual." According to this ongoing study, potential cancer victims were found to differ temperamentally from their fellow students who remained healthy or developed a cardiovascular disorder.

My reaction to cancer followed a course ordained by my temperament. At first I fought it. I sought remedies, a cure. But I soon realized that was not my style. My approach to most serious problems is to turn my back on them. Even with a death-dealing diagnosis, I am disinclined to action. The thought of taking up arms and doing battle with an enemy is foreign to me. I am not a fighter.

I am more likely to lie down and await death. My doctor, who understands the people he takes care of, spared me any more visits to world-famous institutions. He opted instead for making me comfortable.

The body-mind type of mental warfare will continue to draw its adherents. In any case it is harmless. I am likely to lose my hair, develop neuritis, have nausea, insomnia, pain, and generally feel miserable.

Further, I have extreme difficulty in visualizing the talent essential to successful use of the "Happy Warrior" technique whereby the patients visualize their body killing "The Crab" that has taken over.

Max Lerner, in his *Wrestling with the Angel*, takes that

confrontational approach in dealing with two cancers and a heart attack. On many occasions his condition was such that he had not much longer to live—but he bought time with the Norman Cousins/Bernie Siegel mixture of laughter and love.

Most readers have no need to worry at this point. But those of us at or over the biblical span, or going into a hand-to-hand combat with a deadly disease, can take some good advice from Lerner.

And this applies to those who may be giving up on themselves and life for other reasons. You *can* win at the aging game. *Looking death in the eye is only one of the skills we require for successful living.* We age in appearance. We age in attitude. We have a physiological age that is determined by the condition of our arteries. Not to mention a mental age, a social age, and a spiritual age.

But in the long run I do have a rendezvous with death! We'll meet on some disputed barricade.

L IKE WILLIAM BUTLER YEATS, I HAVE SAILED TO Byzantium—the land beyond age. This is my new home. Finally and irrevocably I have been stripped of youth and its powers. My body is devoid of its desires, emotions no longer stirred by the flesh. What filled my life until months ago is gone. Not even memory can bring it back.

I must learn to live in this new world, so different from the one I just left. I am once more a child and must remember growing up. As a child I felt joy, never realizing how infrequent those occasions would be in the years ahead. I went from peak experience to peak experience unaware that soon would come puberty and with it the woe we were promised. Now I am a castrated senior citizen. Not castrated anatomically. In that sense I am intact. I have been castrated by daily shots of Gn-RH, a hypothalamic hormone.

This daily injection reduces my testosterone to a level so low it can barely be detected. It keeps my hormone-dependent tumor and its satellites in my spine under control. I am free of pain, and tests to monitor my status indicate there is very little malignant tissue in my body.

Is this new curse a blessing? Is this death of desire the gift of life? Am I privileged now to return to that Eden of my childhood? I admit that wasn't my first reaction. Yeats tried to put a good face on it, but fought desperately to retain his lust and potency. Byzantium was his haven, but he refused to make the journey.

For the poet Yeats, if not the man, Byzantium was a country for the higher man. Not the risen body but the risen intellect and the risen spirit. Here in a higher evolution stood the true self shorn of the earthy distractions of the body.

It won't wash. There is a Byzantium, but not the one Yeats writes about. There is another country the aging occupy and which we share with children. Its borders are formed by the animal that arises in puberty and subsides with the onset of wisdom. It is a land where seven and seventy are kin. Where there are no concerns other than playing and learning and loving. The inhabitants of this land are in no hurry. Our days are dense with experiences. We have, as the Spanish say, more time than life.

I was an adult once and made the most of it. When I was forty-four I went back to my body and enjoyed its working and its appetites. My body and its drives became the *vis a tergo,* the force behind the total person—father, husband, friend, lover, writer, athlete. I had found my fountain of youth.

There were good times and bad times. Fears, anxieties, depression. Periods of elation, others of despair. Concerns about success and worries about the worst of failures— those with family and friends and those I loved, but through it all I never thought of getting old. Dying, perhaps, but always in the flower of my youth.

Now age has come. Within a season of running I became old. I lost what had fueled my life the past twenty-five years—this age that I am is only partly due to the calendar. Some of this senescence is caused by the therapy for my prostatic cancer. So I have two reasons for curbing the beast within, aging and castration.

Nature, it has been said, makes the most elegant experiments. Time and the removal of one single hormone have made for a unique opportunity to study my own life cycle. Yeats, the poet, has one view. He would put me in a Byzantium where the population has gone on to higher matters. Erikson, the psychiatrist, sees me now enjoying the fruits of the three ages of man: the curiosity of a child, the energy of the adult, and the wisdom of the elder. And with those fruits come the necessary virtues: hope, faith, and charity.

I like that game plan. A new beginning. But this time, not a preparation for a life I would not want to repeat. Rather a preparation for an eternal one. Freed of overpowering urges, no longer in a day-to-day struggle with self and society, emptied of the demons that drove me all those years, I can focus on the work of making a self.

If I were to pick a poet it would not be Yeats; or MacLeish, who made his accommodations with age; or even Frost who refused to yield; it would be Blake. Blake saw all things as holy and was always a child, even to the point of banging on the wall until God answered his call.

Byzantium has begun to look suspiciously like my hometown. It has the same people, the same houses, the same goings and comings. But I am a very wise child seeing things quite differently. The activities and interests of adults mystify me. They appear senseless. It is like watching the TV with the sound off—and suddenly realizing how ridiculous people actually are.

I expect adults will in turn regard me as ridiculous. Actions people might accept in a child may not seem appropriate to a grandfather. I won't be distressed. I am looking forward to new heroes and new adventures. And if you ask me where I've been I'll say "out"; and if you ask me what I've been doing I'll say "nothing."

That's the way we pass the time in Byzantium.

THERE COULD COME A TIME WHEN I AM NO LONger aware of the struggle to live, when I am unable to contribute to decision making. The physicians will be in complete control. This is a situation I dearly wish to avoid. Stories of patients on life support fill the media, although this is less likely to occur with cancer than with other diseases.

Fortunately, this deplorable situation has spurred efforts to avoid it. One such remedy is the "living will." Hospitals and physicians have become interested in this ploy to presumably save the patient. In fact, the game is already lost when life-support tubes are put in place.

My living will, for instance, would express my desire

not to have any therapy when death is clearly inevitable. I have no idea what my last days will be like. I am certain, however, that I don't want to prolong them. I have no interest in lying around in a vegetative state.

Unfortunately physicians, especially younger ones, are trained very much like soldiers. They follow the profession's philosophy, "Fight disease to the bitter end." Unless instructed to the contrary they will use the best medicine and the latest innovations to keep the patient alive.

On the other hand, the older M.D.'s prefer to let nature take its course. They realize they are not omnipotent. If healing is in the cards, God will take care of it.

I can recall the days when pneumonia was labeled "the old person's friend." When life began to ebb, pneumonia delivered the coup de grâce. In the book *The Last Angry Man* we read of the patient's being pushed out on the porch overnight so he would develop pneumonia and die.

This poses an ethical dilemma. Should the M.D. actively aggravate a condition or simply stand by for the inevitable? The living will instructs doctors to cease and desist. When I am no longer able to express my wishes, my family can use this document for instructions to the group.

. . .

THE MOST IMPORTANT PERSON IN MY LIFE, NEXT to myself and my family, is my doctor. Both of us know that it is simply a matter of time until my prostate cancer will deliver me to my Maker. But we also know how important that time is. The length and number and happiness of those days have become my (and his) chief concern.

My doctor is using everything he ever learned or read or experienced to help me through this final period. There have been some bad patches. The old standbys have failed; the new and experimental treatments have been disasters.

Generally, however, our mutual trust and cooperation has made for a satisfactory course. My usual day has become acceptable. I am not what I was. I no longer have sixteen hours of happy, productive living and eight hours of sleep. Mine is a diminished day that includes a long nap and much more sleep than I've ever needed.

Fatigue is a hallmark of cancer. I move less and less. And if you don't use it, you lose it. I push myself to walk and use the stairs. But this is one part of my pact with my physician that I am remiss about. "Life is motion," and I must not forget it.

Appetite is a major problem. Lack of appetite means little or no saliva. Looking at food does not cause my stomach to secrete gastric fluid for digestion. To make up for this, most of my nourishment has to be liquid. I eat "slops." Everything is moist, so I don't have to aid in digestion. Jell-O, custard, milk shakes, soups, pasta, and puddings go down easier than meat and potatoes. I avoid anything I have to chew.

Pain is a subject in itself. My physician's philosophy on pain has changed. Years back doctors were afraid of creating addicts. Now they know cancer patients don't become addicts. Drugs are given early and often. "You should not have any pain," my doctor told me, and he set up a schedule to guarantee that outcome.

Sleep is always welcome. Most waking hours require attention to pain, but beyond that is a certain serenity which accompanies the night hours—whether sleep comes or not.

My companion in all this, and unfortunately also the companion for innumerable other patients, is my doctor. I worry for him. Nearly 60 percent of physicians who specialize in cancer therapy experience burnout. And it is those taking care of patients like me—who cannot be cured—who are most likely to go through what one oncologist has called an emotional "meltdown."

Fortunately, this is a two-way street. Just as my doctor makes it easier for me, I make it easier for him. The dying Anatole Broyard wrote of the patient's responsibility to lighten the doctor's load. Visits should be cheerful, upbeat, and nonthreatening, no matter how things are going.

This is not merely good manners. The positive approach undoubtedly has beneficial effects on our immune systems—and further helps us in this day-to-day living with cancer.

As time passes, I try not to dwell on the usual outcome. Dissatisfaction, discomfort, disease, disability, death. Every patient and his or her physician have to face the inevitable progression.

The Stoic finds this no problem. Stoics concern themselves only with things that are under their control. Hence, their resignation to fate and their main characteristic—*equanimity*. That enables us to face whatever comes without apprehension. To deal with the twists and turns of fate without rancor or despair.

There is one activity of our final days that is practically a duty. A recounting of the family history. My mother died at ninety-one, and many of the events of our past were buried with her. Our last days should be a time for those treasured memories, and for recollection, either in letters or notes or conversations or even by tape recorder.

My mother also had a firm connection with the world—her radio. It was rarely off—day or night, whether she was asleep or awake. I find communication between me and the rest of the world in the same way.

Finally the prospect of death is a spur to meditation and the consolations of religion. It is a time when one gathers one's self just as a rider gathers a horse for a huge leap over a fence or brook.

God enters the equation.

I ONCE VISITED A MENNONITE HOSPITAL WHERE THE medical clinic had a staff equally divided between physicians and clergymen. The Mennonites believe that spiritual health could make an important contribution to physical health. That healing a patient means healing the whole patient.

Those of us in the field of health promotion have largely avoided the subject of spiritual health. True, we have emphasized the global effects of a fitness program. Pointed to the physical and metabolic transformation, to be sure, but a psychological one as well.

We agreed with that implicitly, but we have never explicitly formulated a basic approach to spiritual health; nor have we assigned it to its rightful place in enhancing the quality as well as the quantity of life.

The World Health Organization definition of health, "total physical, mental and social well-being," touches only tangentially on the spiritual, although the development of such well-being certainly has spiritual consequences.

William James, in *The Gospel of Relaxation,* writes of "that blessed internal peace and confidence that wells up from every part of the body of the muscularly well-trained beings and soaks the indwelling soul of him with satisfaction." James said that this was an element of spiritual hygiene that should not be underestimated.

In directing our effort toward spiritual health we cannot confine ourselves to our physical and mental functions. And fortunately we need not worry about the individual's particular belief system. There is a definition of religion that covers all belief systems.

James pointed out in *The Varieties of Religious Experience* that these spiritual experiences have little to do with dogma or theology. The individual in the private recesses of the soul discovers a means to contact an all-good and all-powerful force and is thereby "saved."

This salvation (which comes from the Latin root *salvus,* meaning "safe, healthy") is accompanied by an "assurance state"—the feeling that you are now whole and healed.

At first glance such epiphanies would appear to be gifts. They seem spontaneous and not willed. James would have none of that. Man is incurably religious, he said, and religion is our most important function. We can improve our spiritual health in much the same way we improve our physical health—we must develop the dedication and discipline to do our spiritual exercises and enhance our spiritual strength.

Larry Chapman, a specialist in corporate health programs, suggests a program for optimal spiritual health. It would include:

- *Our ability to discover and define our own basic purpose in life.*
- *Learning how to experience love, joy, peace, and fulfillment.*
- *Learning how to help ourselves and others achieve their full potential.*

These are formidable goals—perhaps difficult enough to discourage people from even starting. Such programs have their equally discouraging counterparts in the physical fitness component as well. Exercise regimens frequently turn out to be exhausting rather than exhilarating, boring rather than fulfilling. They are hard work and make shirkers of would-be believers.

In seeking relatively simple ways to enhance spiritual health, we can turn again to James for an answer. For him, action and feeling went together; and by regulating action, which is under the direct control of the will, we can indirectly control feeling, which is not. Therefore to be cheerful, we must act and speak cheerfully. To feel brave, act as if we *were* brave.

James cites *The Christian's Secret of a Happy Life* by

Mrs. Hannah Whitall Smith as having this lesson on every page. "Act faithfully and you will have faith," Mrs. Smith writes. "It is your purpose God looks at, not your feelings about that purpose; and your purpose is the only thing that you need attend to."

What we must do is relax and free ourselves from worry. And for James, the sovereign cure for worry was religious faith. "The really religious person is unshakable and full of equanimity, and calmly ready for the duty the day brings forth."

When I visited the Mennonites I thought they were ahead of their time, just as William James was ahead of his. But the roots of their clinic go back to a criticism by Plato: "The fault of physicians is they treat the body only and not the soul."

Dad wanted to experience and live each day—not in the past or in the future, but in the present. That was his gift to me—just living life was his gift.

In the last weeks, Dad was eager to hear my stories and experiences, and as I drove home each week, I reflected on my life and fashioned it into a story. Because that is what he taught me. He taught me how to live.

SARAH

I think I'm most thankful to my father for the things he didn't do.

He was never demanding of me.

He never discouraged me.

He never doubted me.

JOHN

> Sell your coat, if necessary, to have your own room.
>
> RALPH WALDO EMERSON

My Family and Me

WHEN THE LATE ROBERT Hutchins, president of the University of Chicago, was asked what he would do differently if given the chance to lead his life over, he replied, "Spend more time with my family."

I would give you six, two, and even against that possibility. And the same likelihood that children would spend more time with their parents.

I write this because of a piece in *The New York Times*

suggesting that my demise will depress my offspring even more, because I didn't visit them enough or exchange family greetings sufficiently.

Let me say first that contemplating death has a salutary effect on a person. I have been called a curmudgeon in some circles but not recently. I have been overwhelmed by how nice people are—and of necessity I am nice in return.

I was always a loner. My family recognized that. "My father likes to have people around when he's reading," one of our daughters remarked. And for years that was the limit of my sociability.

As the cancer grew nearer to the gates I realized this was not enough. A friend told me of his two-week family vacation in a rented house in Hawaii.

It sounded nice to me, so two years ago we spent a week in a large Georgian house in Ireland. Last year we did the same in a spacious house on Long Island.

Although these get-togethers were seemingly unrestricted, they actually were circumscribed. Abby, one of the grandchildren, told her mother, "This isn't a family party, it's a sibling party." And so it was. You had to be of college age to make the roster.

These get-togethers show us at our best, which is what all clans are best at—the relating and shaping of myths. That's why it is so necessary in the late, late stages of life to fashion the myths by which, in our family at least, you will be immortal. A skill we can always call upon.

Those families to whom these concerns present no problem are fortunate. Here, paradoxically, my lifestyle proved to be a vaccine. Being myself allowed them to be themselves. They don't need to be taken care of, for one thing. And in that expression I include the *global* needs of all of us.

Like anyone else they need support, but not in excessive or unusual amounts. Family, education, friends, religion (whatever their version), no gainsaying that. They are, furthermore, all doing their thing and doing it well. No need to worry about having enough time to attain their goals. For them the cliché is true. The travel is more satisfactory than getting there.

Sin, as we must be constantly reminded, is "closing the circle." Our appointed task is to admit everyone—the family and beyond, if possible—to that circle. We do have to take care of people, to like them and to love them. A formidable task.

Edward de Bono, the Cambridge University professor, has reduced this obligation to "respect." Something every one of us is capable of. Love is an emotion; it is, in a sense, a skill and not always available to us. Respect, however, simply requires effort and hence is forever a possibility.

Robert Hutchins did what he did best. He kept his circle open. But I doubt very much that he would have spent more time with his family until it was right and true and just to do so.

Fortunately, the pressure of losing my battle to cancer has made family reunions essential to the evolution of my new self. Without this urgency to get things right, my life would have followed its usual solitary course. Now I am living a new life—and spending more time with a loving and appreciative family.

ANY DEATH CAN GENERATE MEDITATION ON THE great questions in life. But this is especially true when you attend the services of someone to whom you had been strongly attached. This can become the nightly examination of Pythagoras and Ignatius Loyola now taken to a higher level.

By higher level I mean accountability. What is my aim in the time left for me? Am I to become someone different from the person who has answered, "Here!" or "Present!" or "I'm sorry" in attempting to fulfill what seemed my life's role?

Becoming the self I was meant to be is a rule with dangerous implications. It takes me far from the protective shore. "And I have asked to be/Where no storms come," Gerard Manley Hopkins wrote. Becoming a self requires storms. It means turning my back on what Russian theologian Nikolay Berdyayev called herd morality, the system that protects society from explosions and catastrophes.

Spending more time with my family seems like a little thing—but not if done under duress. I recall asking a friend, whose mother was in a nursing home, how much time he spent with her. "As little as possible," he replied.

This may be a gender thing. I know a woman who visited her senile mother in a nursing home every day for over a year. Yet the mother had no idea who she was.

I write of the reverse responsibility because, more often, it is the children who have regrets or a guilty conscience. They feel that they let the parents down.

Now that my life is under pressure I see that family time that fits in with your personality is rewarding. The predominant ectomorphy in me makes for a temperament that wants always to have an escape route. The ectomorphic individual is sensitive to noise, dislikes arguments, avoids confrontations.

When I become uncomfortable, which means vulnerable, I want to have a way out. Hence, I prefer to be "here" and "present," to be physically in touch but not psychologically and socially. And I want the circumstances to be calm and serene.

Fortunately, our family has never been very aggressive. Several of the men have high levels of mesomorphy. They like to speak through their muscles. But they have found outlets in their vocations or avocations. I've known families where the opposite was true. I recall neighbors with five huge sons and no daughters, where the fights were legendary.

Our behavior is normal for our family, just as the neighbors' type of behavior was normal for them. If there is a place for the term *dysfunctional,* it is to be applied to families who fail to deal with their "temperament" in the evolution of their personality.

William Sheldon pointed out that psychopathology, when it exists, is not due to the ectomorphic dominance, but to the deficiency of endomorphy (feeling for people) and mesomorphy (aggressive, type A personality).

Should I then spend my time trying to be a successful ectomorph? Should I accept what my body and in a very real sense my psyche is telling me? Or must I try to strengthen my weaknesses—doing things that go against the grain?

And what of my wife and children, who must wait and watch while I wrestle with these decisions? The experts have suggestions for them:

Be gentle with yourself. Remember the good times.

Give yourself time. The things we have heard about grief and mourning are probably true.

Stay involved with family. Do what our type of family

does best. Stay together and trade family stories. Be open about our experiences.

I recall my feelings at my son's fortieth birthday. It was like that call so frequently heard before a trip, be it for a party, a movie, or a meal. "Come on, we don't have all day." That feeling cuts both ways, for old and young. What I should have done, I can still do. My children also are nearing time to accept the one unique way they are to lead their lives.

The ectomorph in me loves the security of the family. Yet I have fought for my privacy my entire life. "Sell your coat, if necessary, to have your own room," says Ralph Waldo Emerson. Now it is clearly a case of spending more time with the family. But this is a reversal that no other force but my limited life span could bring about. Guilt or shame might have altered my conduct, but only temporarily. I lived the life of the runner-writer with little need for the input of the many lives that impinged on mine.

Now I remain a writer—but no longer a runner. My world has shrunk. I need the support, the laughter, the love that these offspring bring to the family table.

And now I can use what is probably an overused expression, "quality time." What it contains are the relationships, not present before, but now being born between us. They give me moments of happiness, moments that come with the "letting go" I could never achieve in the past.

There should be no regrets on either side. Whatever way time was spent—with the family or not, with the parents or not—it was a natural outcome of the making of a self. It was a part of a much larger project I was carrying on. "Follow your bliss," says Joseph Campbell. *"Amor fati"* (love of fate), says Nietzsche. Carl Rogers has told us this making of the self is done by recognizing the not-self. When Campbell writes of life as a labyrinth, he is telling us of the necessity of following false leads in order to make a successful attempt.

THE BOY WHO RODE ON SLIGHTLY BEFORE HIM sat a horse not only as if he'd been born to it which he was but as if were he begot by malice or mischance into some queer land where horses never were he would have found them anyway. Would have known that there was something missing for the world to be right or he right in it and would have set forth to wander wherever it was needed for as long as it took until he came upon one and he would have known that that was what he sought and it would have been."

The boy riding ahead is John Grady Cole, the young hero of Cormac McCarthy's remarkable novel *All the*

Pretty Horses. The man riding behind is his father, who will die of cancer before the story is finished.

He dies without regrets. His son has found what all of us seek—the absolute certainty of what he was born to be. He is a horseman on a journey that becomes a heroic quest. John Grady, who is as resourceful as Huckleberry Finn and as pure as Billy Budd, tells one lie and thereby unleashes evil and brutality and eventually comes to redemption.

Every parent wants this experience for his or her offspring. Free, of course, of encounters with violence and brutality, but still a trip to discover the self and the other world that somehow influences ours. It matters not what the consuming passion is, save that it must be a passion, some all-absorbing, self-renewing compulsion.

"I must always be at work," said the great Rodin. So it is with anyone who has heard the call within. "Thurber! You're writing again!" James Thurber's wife would admonish him at dinner parties. The same total involvement is expressed in the first line of Norman Maclean's *A River Runs Through It:* "In our family there was no clear line between religion and fly fishing."

This struggle for self-discovery is universal. Life, as Ortega put it, is a desperate struggle to become in fact what you are in design. Knowing your design is the chanciest part. Struggles, no matter how desperate, come easier when you are certain of the goal.

And looking around at my children, now adults doing their thing, I realized that somehow, sometime, somewhere they had gotten the message. Each had found what the horse was to John Grady. Each was doing his or her own thing.

I could see them riding ahead of me—the doctor, the artist, the horse trainer, the teacher, and whatever else they had become. And I knew if they had been born where those possibilities did not exist they would have searched until they found them and would know that was what they sought and it would have been.

THIS SPRING, AFTER FORTY YEARS OF MARRIAGE, I began wearing a wedding ring. It was an announcement that I had finally achieved what Erik Erikson stated was the fifth stage of an individual's eight-stage life cycle, "intimacy."

George Vaillant, a psychiatrist who has studied the subject of male psychological health for over thirty years, gives great importance to attaining intimacy. Vaillant believes that intimacy is a phenomenon that marks the point at which a child becomes an adult.

Vaillant has pointed out that the evolution from one stage to another is neither chronological nor automatic. If a person misses a stage, that person (in Vaillant's subject, the male) must go back and repeat it.

Beyond "intimacy," which Vaillant defines as living successfully with a non–family member for ten years or more, there are more virtues a person must achieve. Identity, caring, in Erikson's term "generativity," and finally, wisdom. Each one of these stages represents, as does intimacy, a crisis. It is possible to fail them individually or serially and to have to repeat them as well.

We must, therefore, succeed in each one of Erikson's eight stages. In that way we evolve in a progression that begins with the raw material of temperament, grows into a distinctive personality, and finally achieves character. That assures our destiny.

Vaillant's studies have emphasized certain characteristics that portend a good end result. Competence in adolescence is more important than IQ. A good relationship with parents is helpful when we reach our fifties. Our feelings toward our siblings become decisive to happiness in our sixties.

We have to succeed in every stage. And this success is measured against what is possible and potential in us. It is not a competition against others. But this concept points out the danger of negatives in weighing our strengths and weaknesses. The challenges we accept or that others propose to us must be possible.

The most difficult progression surely has to be from child to adult. The qualities needed for intimacy are not prominent in a child. Patience, discipline, dedication, compassion, selflessness are hard-won virtues. They do not come easily or automatically. And some of us are very slow learners.

Our society, of course, reflects failures at every one of Erikson's stages and Vaillant's as well. Few of us have no need for courses in remedial living. We have to make up for deficiencies in the evolutionary pattern of our lives.

My marriage satisfied Vaillant's definition of success in intimacy; but despite that I came to recognize that I had never made the transition from child to adult. In my writings I had extolled being *childlike*, which is something to be desired. It is quite another matter, however, to be *childish*.

By rights my marriage should have foundered long ago, but my wife made up for both of us. She is a definition of why relationships work. Others marry or have relationships who are not that fortunate. Still children, they are frequently living with a person who is more child than adult as well.

After forty-nine years I passed through another life crisis to become the adult husband I was meant to be.

· · ·

ENTER STAGE IN MY LIFE WITH CANCER ARE the physical symptoms that heckle me from when I rise until I go to bed. Symptoms are what my body tells me ruins its day. Pain, fatigue, weakness, light-headedness are things only I can know.

I do my best to minimize these problems. My doctors help as well. The pain is fairly well controlled. Weakness is another story. The cortisone that suppresses my immune response has a catabolic effect—a breakdown of my leg muscles. Exercising to improve muscle tone is a losing battle for me; like Sisyphus I have to run just to stay in place. The stairs at home are, as they say in the Tour de France, "beyond category." I have to stop twice on the ascent and be very careful on the way down. I have my own exercise spa—a stationary bicycle, an arm ergometer, and some dumbbells. However, my defenses daily are pushed back. Each day I do less and less.

One incapacity is my difficulty getting out of bed. It seems almost incredible that getting up is so difficult. I have to invent ingenious ways to get into the upright position. In fact, changing position in bed, getting out of a chair, and other maneuvers have made me find creative solutions.

Fatigue causes different problems. The first is acceptance. I take it for granted that all men are capable of a specific twenty-four-hour day which includes eight to nine hours of sleep. I now find that I need a nap every day.

Unfortunately, I don't want to waste my remaining time on naps, and I skip more naps than I take. I need more than eight hours' sleep. I usually get nine hours.

Husbanding my strength in this way has proven helpful. I am, however, delighted to get horizontal at 10:00 P.M. There is no feeling during the entire day quite like that feeling. It's like being airborne, weightless. Suddenly living requires no effort. I go back to what I do best, thinking and writing.

The light-headedness is always a surprise and can be dangerous. If I arise suddenly, my blood pressure drops and I fall to the ground. I have the bruises as evidence.

This symptom can be prevented. Sitting forward on the chair or bed and tensing before arising will get me through the day without alarming everyone around me.

There is an enormous difference between being sick and being well. I watch from my window and see people young and old striding along the boardwalk. I have become aware of the strength and vitality in these bodies and contrast it with my own capabilities.

Their élan vital they take for granted. And all the while I have to plan meticulously to get out of bed, to go up and down stairs, to get off the toilet. I am not surprised anymore that elderly people break their hips. I am surprised it doesn't happen more often.

Having cancer is having precipitate aging. It accelerates changes so that they take days instead of decades. Suddenly I am an invalid. I am grateful for the help I get from others.

Accepting that help is completely foreign to my personality. But a four-story home is not the ideal for a cancer patient. So my family does the stairs for me. My memory, long a difficulty for me, now affects them also. They have to make the trips for books and paper and pen. They run and fetch like pet spaniels. They replenish supplies at the store, bring the morning *Times* and coffee, stand by to assist me out of the ocean.

I not only need them, I delight in their attention. We are a very close family but have had difficulty expressing that closeness. Now I have become a focus that brings all of us together. We are one.

My wife, who has charge of my medications, and I have become the center of this galaxy of twelve sons and daughters who orbit around us. They call, they visit, they express solicitude. There are no minor planets or stars in this sky. I cannot justify being that important, but I know they are.

. . .

MY DIALOGUE WITH DEATH IS A SOLITARY pursuit. My day involves all the usual activities. I have to deal with the usual worries, cares, and duties that I had before my disease changed my life.

Fortunately, solitude is favorable to me. I enjoy being alone. Schopenhauer describes this difference in people. There are those who can tolerate pain but not boredom—they are a race apart from me. And there are those who can tolerate boredom but not pain.

Ennui has never been my problem. My physical and spiritual energies may have limitations, but not my mental ones. My brain is tireless. True, you might point out my dry periods at work. You might think I suffer from writer's block.

It is not so. Work is continually in progress. Nothing may be put down on paper, but in the subconscious I am composing columns to come. Ray Bradbury has said that he never had writer's block. He might not write for some months, but pages and pages were being stored up in his brain.

So death may not be in my conscious mind. I may not hear a dialogue between me and my psyche. But I am confident that I continue to have insights on my condition. Ideas, old and new, are being inspected while I am unaware of it.

There are, of course, the products of an active solitary state. The extent to which I can understand death comes about by following thinkers and writers who were experts in solitude. Almost all of these individuals look to the reverie for inspiration. So they utilized time each day to reach this state. Mind you, this was in good times, although the creative person is always under pressure.

Reveries on death, however flawed, should be valuable. I can dovetail my own reactions with those of the people whose books populate my library. What I discovered was that these were the same people who illuminated my running experience. Every race was a learning experience. In cancer, every day is a learning experience.

And as with running it is a necessary procedure. First the experience, then the discovery of its meaning. The contemplative is always trying to find out what happened. And one has to do this alone.

In such a period, addition of other people is usually harmful. Creativity is not by committee. Now more and more of my time is spent alone. My thoughts are not focused only on death. I'm thinking about the people I will leave behind and my responsibility for them.

My dialogue is "I" talking to "me." The reason: something to leave my children and my children's children.

This new self amazes me. The experts help in finding the self—and self-descriptions are usually quite accurate, if a little exaggerated. But we are truly as my friend Brenda Euland says—multiple selves. Facing death I am liable to expose these selves successfully. As I study their various reactions from Thoreau to Mishima I see yet another of my selves on view.

In common is pleasure in the solitary state, and complete honesty in the experience. At such times I am not sure whether the urgency is positive or negative. What I am sure of is that there must be an awareness of the proximity of death. People are writing about death who are not dying. If you are going to write about death you should at least be sick.

L IFE IS A TERMINAL ILLNESS," WRITES SAMUEL Beckett. When my prostate cancer spread into my bones this process went on "fast forward." I was forced to deal with the stages of death and dying.

The first is *denial.* When I heard the cancer diagnosis, I had a feeling of disbelief. This can't be happening to me. It was difficult to believe that yesterday was a normal day and now I was dealing with a fatal disease.

Next, for me, was fear. A *fear,* I might say, close to

panic. I had a week of sleepless nights until I realized that, for now anyway, I felt the same as last month.

What usually follows is *anger*. Dr. Edward Creagan, an oncologist at the Mayo Clinic who has written on this problem, says that the anger may be directed at oneself, a spouse, a physician, or the system. I must admit I spent no time in this stage. Being a runner, I accepted no excuses. This was the luck of the draw.

After that comes *bargaining*. We recognize this from adolescence, when we make a pact with a "higher power." We promise to do better, return to the righteous life, or contribute to the community in exchange for a reprieve.

Next comes *depression*. When it becomes evident that the treatments are not effective—and those waiting to be tried not much better—depression ensues. Patients tend to give up. They become withdrawn and lose energy. They have no enthusiasm for their daily tasks.

During these stages I spent most of my time searching for a cure. There were newsletters and support groups that had information on various programs around the country. I spoke with or visited experts at the most prestigious institutions. I learned that every now and then they had an exceptional result—but these exceptional results were truly exceptions.

Meanwhile, I was being taught how to deal with the inevitable. I was gradually coming into the final stage, *ac-*

ceptance. Dr. Creagan describes this as a complete reversal of attitude. The attempts to find a magic cure or reprieve from the disease decrease. Patients become less focused on their illness, tests, and treatment. They go back to living each day to the fullest.

Dr. Creagan tells the story of a prominent member of his community. This man was obsessed with finding a cure for his terminal cancer and had investigated treatment options throughout the world. When he finally accepted the reality of his situation, his conversations centered on his golf game and his family instead of some new treatment.

Acceptance, as difficult as it is for the patient, may be even more difficult for the family. The cancer victim, having won this peace, has to deal with loving relatives who are still engaged in the search for a cure.

I recall something my sister said to me when she was getting chemotherapy for her fatal cancer. "I wouldn't take this, George, except I want the family to be sure I did everything."

For the cancer patient, "doing everything" is reaching acceptance, or what Friedrich Nietzsche called *amor fati*—the love of our fate, whatever that turns out to be.

I was the youngest of the first group, the "big kids," and you were my distant protector—from the teasing of my older brothers, making sure I was included in the games. . . . I remember the day I was swimming in the ocean and had gone out too far. The waves were pulling me out, crashing on me, and I was terrified. And then I heard your voice calling to me.

During the years you were gone I tried to stay angry, to shut you out; I thought I had lost you, that you were lost. But you came back, and in that last year you gave me your final gift, one I had been waiting for but had forgotten. I looked into your eyes, as blue as the ocean you loved, and I saw you off in the distance, swimming toward me, protecting me . . . and I was not afraid.

NORA

I am no longer concerned with good and evil. What concerns me is whether my offering will be acceptable.

ROBERT FROST

A Little Help from My Friends

TODAY AS I LISTENED ON MY SHORTwave radio I heard about the dolphins in the Bahamas. These dolphins were helping people cope with cancer and depression and a number of other things. Their effectiveness depended on "pure love."

I wasn't interested in how effective they were. Pure love, however, interests me. I have it in my house. Every day someone in my family manifests his or her complete and utter concern for me. They do not purr like dolphins, but they are always ready for any trouble.

Dying, as with Amiel, may be extremely slow. It should not be so with prostate cancer—not, at least, when symptoms persist, or pain, fatigue, and wasting occur. Still I may become a nuisance if things go on too long. Maybe I'll have the time and strength to compare my family to the dolphins.

My friend Fred Lebow, president of the New York Road Runners Club, came to a recent postrace party and told me that this was his third Last Seder since he was diagnosed with a brain tumor. I thought about his survival and my longevity and said, "Fred, people will be getting mad at us. All that sympathy but no evidence that we are going to die." There'll come a time when friends and family will return to their pursuits. And we'll return to the dolphins for the pure love we need.

WE DIE OF OUR ENTIRE LIFE. WE BRING TO those final hours a temperament, a personality, a character, an evolving self different in various ways from any other self in the universe.

But for all that, there are specific ways in which we try to achieve what psychiatrist Robert Jay Lifton calls "symbolic immortality."

The first is *biological*—the family, and by extension a group and a community. I shall attest to the increasing importance of my wife and children and grandchildren.

And I confess this was not true in the past. Now we have family and friends every week. These past two years we had week-long family reunions. I have the sense I will live on through them.

Symbolic immortality can also be sustained by *religious faith*. Ahead lies an existence on a higher plane. We will leave this profane life with all its trials and enjoy eternal happiness. For most of my life I felt immortality held the opposite, the eternal tortures of hell. Now I'm on the fence. A ninety-year-old woman wrote me that she believed "death is the ultimate peak experience."

More pragmatic people find immortality in their *creativity*. Here works, teaching, influence on others take on a life of their own. This is part of the formula in the Old Testament: to sire a son, to write a book, to plant a tree, to build a house. Planting a tree binds one with the eternal nature around us. I write this in my living room and in the presence of a vast sea that occupies half my horizon. How long before me did this water mass exist and how long after I'm gone will it still be here? Yet I am part of that and indeed of the entire universe. I have been an event and continue in some way to participate.

Lifton's final approach to symbolic immortality is *psychic*. It is the mystical experience. It brings into play an expansion of our self-conscious self. We accept that there are other and greater realities. It could be described as transcendence or being transformed. It is totally experiential and we have only the testimony of those who have been there that such states exist. We must seek them in our own way.

As my time shortens I have a choice: I can look for therapy for my cancer that will add months or years to my life; or I can devote what time I have left to studying this confrontation with death. I can look to the people I have read and admired. I can find out how they handled their last days. What I should know is how people who resembled me, at least in temperament and personality, thought, felt, and acted when death became their immediate future.

DYING IS A TRANSFORMING EXPERIENCE. WE need no more evidence of this than the last days of Henry David Thoreau.

Thoreau was a difficult person to like. Robert Louis Stevenson, after looking at Thoreau's portrait, made this perceptive assessment:

"Thoreau's thin, penetrating large nose in fact conveys some hint of the limitations of his character. Thoreau is not easy, not ample, not urbane, not even kind. It was much easier for Thoreau to say no than yes."

Even those quite close to Thoreau took this view. "I love Henry," said one of his friends, "but I cannot like him; and as for taking his arm, I should as soon think of taking the arm of an elm tree."

Thoreau had an adversarial view of life. He was energized by causes. But for all that, he was a model of Emerson's Transcendentalist. He was not a good citizen. He was the consummate "outsider."

Approaching these final years I was no different from Thoreau. I did not wish my neighbor ill, but I didn't wish him well, either. My writings and lectures preserved a moat between me and my audiences.

My penetrating big-nosed face should have alerted my listeners as Thoreau's did Stevenson. Here was a person who lacked the breeding of the Brahmins. A person who was attempting to make up for obvious defects by creating a new person.

This being so, the change in Thoreau in his final year is important to me. In the months he took to die, an entirely different Thoreau took residence in Concord. This was not a "foxhole conversion." It was not a recantation of his philosophy. What Thoreau demonstrated was an entirely different approach to his fellow man.

The dying Thoreau is a new Thoreau. Peace, pleasure, and acceptance became part of his day. "Yes! This a beautiful world," he says, "but shall I see a fairer."

And quite new to him, or at least to his consciousness, was the kindliness of his neighbors. His sister Sophia writes, "It is really pathetic the way in which the town was moved to minister to his comforts. Total strangers sent grateful messages remembering the good he had done them."

Thoreau's response: "I should be ashamed to stay in this world after so much has been done for me, I could never repay my friends." How much that expresses my own feelings. I am humbled by letters and gifts I have received since my physical deterioration became known.

Fortunately, Thoreau had reached the stage of acceptance. He refused to see any more doctors. At that late stage, he told Bronson Alcott that there was as much comfort in perfect disease as in perfect health; the mind always conformed to the condition of the body.

Be assured that death can be a positive and transforming experience—if you accept the conditions it imposes. For Thoreau it was final acceptance when he wrote, "It is just as good to be sick—just as good to have a poor time as a good time."

His goals changed. The theme of death as something natural and acceptable fills his letters. In one he writes, "You ask particularly about my health. I suppose you know that I have not many months to live; but, of course, I know nothing about it. I may add that I am enjoying existence as much as ever, and regret nothing."

One townsman who dropped in for a visit two months

prior to Thoreau's death said that he had never spent an hour with more satisfaction. He had never seen a man dying with more pleasure and peace.

Yet he always had time for a flash of the Thoreau wit. A few days before the end a visitor said to him, "You seem so near the brink of the dark river, that I almost wonder how the opposite shore may appear to you."

To which Thoreau responded, "One world at a time."

WHEN ANATOLE BROYARD, THE LONGTIME book reviewer for *The New York Times,* died of prostate cancer, he left behind a description of his encounter with death. As an admirer of Broyard's writings and now a fellow victim of prostate cancer, I see him as an example of how best to deal with the process of dying.

In many ways I resemble him. I am a writer. Like Broyard, "all my friends are wits." And, as with Broyard, who received special attention in an emergency room, there are people who are grateful for my writings and wish to do something in return.

In fact, Broyard was the perfect patient: "There is an etiquette to being sick. I never act sick with my doctor." Broyard was a southerner with southern manners. I know of many such polite patients. A physician told me about his experience taking care of a fellow physician dying of prostate cancer. "When I visit him," he said, "he never mentions his disease."

What stands out about Broyard is his enormous consideration for others and his sense of humor. He died the way he lived, in his own fashion. "A man dies of his entire life," wrote the French philosopher Charles Peguy. Broyard demonstrated that.

My cancer is teaching me how to die. There is a progression of feelings I must go through before I accept the inevitable. The last thing I want is to have friends avoid me. If I am in agony I don't want to visit it on anyone else. My task is to find the humor in all this suffering. Be assured, it is there. The novelist J. F. Powers once said, "Life is so funny that something will crack you up at your wife's funeral."

It happens every day with cancer.

ENRI-FREDERIC AMIEL TOOK A LONG TIME TO die. But fortunately this nineteenth-century Swiss professor recorded his experience in the 17,000-page journal he kept for over thirty years. His fatal illness, a struggle with bronchial disease, is first noted in his entries years before his death, and the entries follow its course to his eventual demise.

I should not look for humor in Amiel's report on his death.

Seven years before his death from lung disease in 1881,

he wrote in his journal, "To die quickly is a privilege, I shall die by inches." And then just a little later he has this entry: "I shall die by suffocation and the suffocation has begun."

The quick death of Broyard was not for him.

In the ensuing years he continues to write about pain and death and the loss of health. A typical report: "For three to four hours last night I struggled against suffocation and looked death in the face . . . I shall die by choking."

As his condition worsens his journal becomes more spiritual—more about his mind and spirit and less about his body. His purpose, he makes evident, is to make his particular situation applicable universally. "All personal events, all particular experiences are to me texts for meditation, facts to be generalized into laws, realities to be reduced to ideas."

For Amiel most things could be reduced to duty—a duty freely accepted, although he admits that indecision is his principal defect.

In his final year, 1881, he looks more closely at death. "We dream alone, we die alone, we inhabit the last resting place alone." But before that occurs he finds solace: "There is nothing to prevent us from opening our solitude so monologue becomes dialogue, reluctance becomes docility, renunciation passes into peace."

He writes of the "drowning" that was gradually taking over his waking hours. We see how important religion was to his response. His was not too specific. Like the historian Arnold Toynbee, he was looking for a maximum of religion with a minimum of dogma.

Amiel encapsulates his view in one entry: "Be good, pious, patient and heroic, faithful and devoted, humble and charitable; the catechism which has taught you these things is beyond the reach of blame."

He kept all this inside, using the journal to empty his mind. He saw no reason to inflict what was happening to him on his friends. His dialogue was with God, not with his colleagues and students.

I began with that same resolve. I was not going to visit my sufferings on family and friends. I was not long in breaking that vow. My internal support was too weak to be capable of dealing alone with my prostate cancer and its progression.

Still we are remarkably similar. My life is the life of the mind. And, as with Amiel, "Indecision is my principal defect." I have no journal, but for the past twenty-five years I've written a weekly column—a suitable alternative. And now I am dealing with a foe who will eventually take me off this planet—"The King of Terrors."

Amiel answers this threat with reliance on religion. He finds the qualities that will bring him through those last days; the Catechism calls them the "Gifts of the Holy Ghost." He finds uses for them all.

And once more we have someone trumpeting the absolute value of experience. When your time comes you will understand. Meanwhile, despite what we say or write, you are seeing "through a glass darkly."

Death is not going to give up its secrets cheaply. Reading the words of those intimate with this stage in life is helpful, and through them we get glimmerings of real action.

To an extent, I can exchange ideas with Amiel. I can, perhaps, feel the presence of the Holy Ghost. I may even sin against the Holy Ghost—by reading Amiel instead of writing my own thoughts. Dying with Henri Amiel is an uplifting experience. Events over a century ago in Geneva become part of a universal me. The catechism is simple. Do your duty, let God do His.

The translation of Amiel's suffocation into my own pain is like all translations—it suffers. But of those who take the time to describe the encounter with "The King of Terrors," Amiel may have as much to tell us as anybody.

Death calls upon a variety of responses. The quiet, mild Swiss professor showed that such happenings are unpredictable. What happened to him is described in the theological texts as a "state of grace."

The thought occurs that the same phenomenon will occur with me. Faced with death I will rise to the occasion. And through word or deed make others proud.

A FEW YEARS AGO, I WAS STANDING ON THE PODIUM of a Unitarian church in San Diego answering questions following a talk on "What's New in Training, Nutrition, and Injuries." The runners in front of me were asking questions that went deeper than training for races, carbo-loading, and exercise-induced asthma. "What are your main concerns?" someone asked. "What would you do differently?" queried another. "Have you become more religious?" asked someone else. They were looking at me as an elder and wondered what happened after a lifetime of running and with time running out.

I was silent for a time. Then, my arms in front of me, palms upward as if in supplication, I looked heavenward and asked, "Did I win?"

It was the question of a schoolboy being asked by someone just a few years short of being truly old. I have spent my life playing a game in which I am not sure of the rules or the goal. At this point I was asking of whoever is in charge the big question: "Did I win?"

Although I am seventysomething, I still wonder whether I played this game of life well enough to win. It is so difficult to know what really mattered. It's as if all my life was spent studying for a final examination, and now I am not sure just what was important and what wasn't.

Did I win? Does any of us know? Is there anything we have done that assures us we have passed the test? Can we be sure we did our best at whatever it was that we were supposed to do?

It is a tough call. Obituaries are filled with achievements that mark those we think of as successful. But obituaries tend to conceal biographies, and those biographies tell us the deficiencies and defeats of even the great and near great.

So we don't know. Alexander Woollcott once said to his fellow alumni of Hamilton College, "Some of you are successes and some are failures. And only God knows which are which." Even with clear evidence of weakness or wrongdoing, of having a guilty conscience or none at all, we may be looking at someone who passed the test, someone who knew and did what is necessary for the winning of life.

Each one of us is an experiment-of-one. Each is a unique, never-to-be-repeated event. Our talents vary. Our defeats are our own. Our environments offer special challenges. We evolve from a constant interaction between instinct and will, between emotions and reason, between environment and good fortune. Life, like it or not, is a handicap event, and a winner may finish deep in the pack.

"Did I win?" is indeed the question of a schoolboy. It is the question of someone unfamiliar with the rules, someone who doesn't know the inner workings of the game. But it is also the question of someone who tried as hard as he could. At an age when I should know all the answers, I am still that young boy. Seventysomething should be the age of wisdom. Everything should be clear. But there are still too many missing pieces.

I think of my sins and the passions that occasioned them and suspect they were not all that important. What is important is the lying and the cruelty and the greed, the daily obstacles to making my life what it could have been.

When Robert Frost was in his sixties he wrote, "I am no longer concerned with good and evil. What concerns me is whether my offering will be acceptable."

Frost wrote some hard things—and this may be the hardest and truest of all. The answer to the question "Did I win?" is "Yes, if your offering is acceptable."

I am still working on mine.

S INCE I STARTED THIS CHRONICLE OF MY FINAL ILL-ness, I have received a number of letters from readers offering support. This solidarity is part of the human condition. People tend to work together.

Very occasionally a writer contributes more than advice and prayers; the writer offers an experience that alters every perception of death. My letter came from a woman who was eleven years old when her sister died at twenty-one. She wanted me to know that her sister's last words were, "How beautiful." Nothing I have read before or since has given me more peace.

In these last days, I would like to exhibit the acceptance of Thoreau, the patience of Amiel, the humor of Broyard, and the honesty of Robert Frost.

But with all those qualities and the help they gave, this report of the twenty-one-year-old tells me what we've been told over the centuries. Death is not the end.

My father found fame and he found its limits.

He searched until he found only pain and when

his pain embraced him, he embraced it back.

It humbled him, it sweetened him.

Grounded in this way he became

a healer and he began to heal his children.

ANDREW

The Cancer Is Winning

WHEN YOUR PHYSICIAN announces that you have a certain amount of time to live, take it with a grain of salt. Stewart Alsop put this skepticism in his book *Stay of Execution*. His anticipated course ending in death just didn't come about.

I am going through the same experience. Both my doctor and I gave up on orthodox therapy, and all the complementary (unorthodox) treatments like shark cartilage. Nationally known researchers gave me two months or more to live. The chances of their various drugs to help me were very slim.

I took one stab at curative treatment. I went to the National Institutes of Health and spent a miserable week in a Bethesda motel barely able to walk, my appetite reduced to two cups of yogurt daily.

The waiting room for the prostate cancer clinic gave me hope. The men in the other chairs were successes. My chance, I was told, was 30 percent. After a week I took back my chips. It wasn't worth feeling that bad for my remaining months.

The alternative, however, was not much better. I had no appetite, and pain filled my days and interfered with my sleep. My days passed in a fugue state. My physician had yet to tell me how I would die and I didn't recall a patient of mine expiring from prostate cancer. I was in the dark, therefore, as to what was coming next.

With my hormone therapy, I had gone six years with my cancer quiescent. Then it went on fast forward. My bone scan was filled with evidence of tumor. It looked like a target in a shooting gallery. I became a prisoner of pain.

I was about to concede to an accelerated, painful death when I got a call from a physician friend on the West Coast. His advice was succinct: Take enough morphine to relieve the pain. Take enough cortisone to slow your reaction to the tumor. "That will get you six months," he said, "then we'll talk about it again."

He was right on. The cancer, without any medication directed against the malignant cells, continues to grow, and my tests worsen. I have a blood transfusion from time to time. But somehow the cortisone has prevented the brushfire I expected.

But morphine? Over the years that had been our absolute last resort as physicians. Doctors thought the use of opiates (particularly morphine and Demerol) should be limited; otherwise patients become addicted.

Morphine and other opiates are now the first line of defense. One recent TV documentary showed a woman in a hospital ward, who was identified as being on morphine, doing the *New York Times* crossword puzzle.

My physician explained this new approach. "First, you must have no pain." It is an old precept in medicine that it takes a much lower dose to prevent pain than it does to relieve it.

The morphine is everything my friend claimed it would be. It has been a godsend. I take one dose in the morning and one at night. Pain is now no more than a rumor. I have trouble remembering what it was like.

Why? We must never underestimate the hidden psychological strengths we have. "The body has a head."

There is a discipline called psychoimmunology, and the placebo effect, religion, and other sources of resistance to disease must be cultivated.

But also there is science. Cortisone earned the Nobel Prize for the Mayo Clinic's Philip Hench. It had wonderful effects on arthritis, and only later on was it found that this was not permanent. Old-timer physicians who remember that era are more likely to use cortisone in a variety of ailments despite its temporary characteristics. It is also evident that all the evils that beset humanity have an element of immune disease and allergy. Whether you have pneumonia, cancer, or advancing age, attention paid to an allergic response will pay off.

How long will I be on death row? It is becoming uncertain. My old-timer knows his steroids. He went through the initial euphoria of Hench's discovery. He knows what can be expected and for how long.

My doctor is ignoring the tumor. He is a realist. Cure is out of the question, so he settles for comfort. For me it's a new lease on life. I thought the jig was up, the die was cast. All I wanted was my blanket and my binkie.

Old man that I was, I was willing to settle for the life of a child—friends, books, ice cream, my radio, and an ocean to swim in and to face the horizon as I sit on my porch. This new program gives me that. The tests con-

tinue to worsen, and what people see of me may be a fa-
çade, a Potemkin village, ready to collapse any day. That
may well happen. Still I rush along with no signs of addiction, always trying "to make every day count."

Treatment of pain has become a specialty in medicine.
Other diseases besides cancer cause intolerable (and in-
tractable) pain. The dying poet Rilke, who had leukemia,
reported that his pain was unbearable and efforts by
physicians were failures. Pain became part of his life.

This was in part due to the fact that he was an ectomorph like me and had an extremely low pain threshold.
I once said my threshold was at the level of a firm hand-
shake. That's the time for morphine.

Despite the availability of morphine and its recom-
mendation by the cancer unit of the World Health Organization, it is estimated that 25 percent of all cancer
patients die without the relief of severe pain.

There is payment for these good things. Cortisone destroys muscles. My quads are shot. The marathoner who
ran Boston twenty-one times has to go up stairs one step
at a time. I can no longer run. A twenty-minute walk is a
major project. When I swim, a member of the family accompanies me in case I need someone to help me get out.

A small price for what I am getting in return.

. . .

I OFTEN RECEIVE PHONE CALLS FROM PEOPLE WITH prostate cancer. They know I have this form of cancer and seek advice as to treatment. One major problem, for those with advanced cancer, is pain. Many have pain, particularly at night, that consumes their energies, spoils their sleep, and generally makes life miserable.

I go through life pain-free day after day while my fellows are suffering. The fact is that pain is unnecessary. It can be prevented by simple measures. And in other countries, particularly England and Australia, many cancer programs are based on this philosophy. The patient is kept, to the extent that it is possible, pain-free.

Sometimes this requires more sophisticated methods of pain relief. Pain clinics have a variety of ways to remove pain from a patient's daily life. This is especially true in terminal prostate cancer, where pain is a very prominent feature.

A doctor can certainly throw up his hands about reversing this process in any way. The tumor cells inexorably eat away at the bones, creating pressure on the nerves. I do not expect my M.D. to change this, but he should be able to relieve my pain. He should improve the quality of the remainder of my life with his use of the amount and type of painkiller.

Generally this thought does not seem to occur to the caretakers. The Young Turks looking for cures don't attend to the issue of pain at all. Old-timers who accept the inevitable are concerned that the suffering patient doesn't wheedle some opiates out of them, because in the old way of thinking, doctors were warned against addiction.

My cousin and I both have cancer. We compare symptoms. We help each other. He is in constant pain; I have relief because of my doctor's philosophy. My cousin is visiting. He goes home with some of my morphine. His wife calls—we have passed a miracle. No cure, but relief of pain.

The primary reason for pain in cancer, says a writer to *The Lancet,* a British medical journal, is opiophobia, a fear of using these drugs by M.D.'s—plus, of course, a lack of education in caring for cancer patients. The rule: No patient should live with unrelieved pain when relief is possible.

THE MAN WHO COMPLETED TWENTY-ONE BOS-ton Marathons cannot get out of bed.

This morning I fell getting out of bed. My legs are too weak to walk in an upright position. It took my wife and me an hour before I was sitting on the side of the bed and bleeding sites had been dressed.

I now fall on a regular basis. I usually land on my head. There is a general clatter and the rest of the family rushes to my aid. There should be a short book on *The*

Physics of Cancer. It would deal with small but important items—getting on and off the toilet, for instance, climbing stairs, getting out of bed, swimming in the ocean.

Sounds unnecessary, but the marathoner may go almost imperceptibly from independence to a wheelchair. Being wheeled around is quite pleasant once you get over swallowing your pride.

Each day brings new problems. Not as acute and memorable as my weekly races, but new and of the stuff that teaches—experiences that reach deep and leave an imprint.

This is the way my books were written. It was the way I wrote books on running. First, to believe what I was writing about was important; and second, to base it on actual experience. In writing, as in any other successful activity, you need inside information. Too often a reporter calls me who wants to write a piece on the marathon. Impossible. *I've* been there, *I* should write it.

So it is with my struggle with cancer. This day-to-day duty in the front lines has given me firsthand information. I have, for one thing, a gradual loss of functions. Will I get to ride my bike again? Perhaps. I am convinced, however, that running will never again fill any part of my day.

Mostly I await the future. The future today is filling

time until it's 9:00 P.M. and I can go to bed. I would never have believed lying flat would feel so good. Nor that getting out of bed would be so difficult.

My life nevertheless is like a game of chess. I am up against a master. The conclusion is inevitable. But the nature of the checkmate is still a mystery.

TRADITIONALLY, WOULD-BE PHYSICIANS STUDY Latin in order to understand the Latin roots of the names of the diseases they study. Occasionally the result is confusing. An example is the word *necrobiosis,* used by Professor Boyd in his book on pathology, which was required reading in virtually every medical school in New York.

Our professor of pathology was Jean Oliver, a man with great bushy eyebrows who so intimidated the class that no one would ask a question, so he installed a box for us to use. One day he came in ranting about Boyd's use of the word *necrobiosis:* "What can he mean?" he asked rhetorically. Not one of the cowering students would dare to answer him. *Necro* = death, *bios* = life. "How can they coexist?" Now I know.

Necrobiosis is entropy. It is what cancer is doing to me, the gradual breaking down over a period of time. It begins, we would suppose, with birth, but the curve probably doesn't start to descend until the age of thirty.

Entropy occurs, cancer or no. It is impossible to stop entropy, but it is possible to slow the rate.

I check daily for such changes. Yesterday, my physician noticed my foot slaps when I walk. Today it is evident that I have a footdrop. My left foot won't respond to orders. Somewhere in its course the nerve to the foot is being interfered with.

So it goes. Some patients and physicians try to slow this process with drugs. My inclination has been to observe it. When the time comes, I'll try to restore a new balance. For today, *necros* is ahead of *bios*.

The élan vital is my counterbalance—Dr. Oliver would be proud that I remember his words of fifty years ago. The life principle enters the equation. Cancer causes noise in the system and the software program fails to operate.

The malignant cell under the microscope looks more energetic than less—but the story is the opposite. It cannot operate without proper direction.

Entropy is a concept that seems interesting but irrelevant. In actuality entropy on close study indicates the true nature of *necro-bios*. What is happening to me is important. Study of this process could be quite productive.

Claude Berner generalized on entropy using the concept of homeostasis, maintenance of our internal milieu. As we age, our bodies find this more difficult to do. We cope by slowing down. As we age we handle height, heat, cold, dehydration less well. But breakdown is quite another thing.

Examples of acute entropy abound, but it is difficult to point to specific individuals who clearly demonstrate this process. My own course, however, is an example of the subject and what cancer brings to the situation.

NOW THAT MY MUSCLES ARE DISAPPEARING and fatigue is a constant presence, I am reminded of plans I had and never followed. Previously, there was always time. Everyone, even those in England and Ireland, was no more than a phone call away. The races I had somehow never run were, with the slightest urging, ready to have me in as a guest celebrity.

There is so much I haven't done.

What is Venice like? And does Florence so overshadow it? And at home, the Grand Canyon and the Tetons? How about an epic bike ride from Seattle to Ocean Grove?

I am like Thoreau, who traveled widely in Concord. But even there I am at fault. How much of Manhattan have I missed? All the shows and museums, the tourist attractions. I lived three decades in New York City with blinders on.

In some ways, this is the most unexpected consequence

of cancer. With heart attacks, the victim, quite often, is completely functioning only minutes or hours or days before.

There is no long prodromal period for many with coronary disease. How often we read of sudden death on a vacation—or a demise during squash or tennis or jogging. Health and energy distinguish the life of the cardiac even while the arteries are clogging up.

So cancer brings its special problems, inertia and gradual destruction. "Crumbling is not an instant's Act," wrote Emily Dickinson. I am finding out that fortunately this slow process brings with it the desire to meditate on its significance.

Slow dying has its advantages. Learning of cancer eight years ago led first to therapy to hold it in check, and when it accelerated I was left with places and events I always planned to visit or experience.

Now my daily battle with cancer has pushed even those thoughts and wanderings to the background. I arise, follow a schedule within my capabilities, then retire. Anything more is too much. My chances to enjoy the pleasures and treasures around me have gone.

The columnist Stewart Alsop, in his *Stay of Execution*, gives me an example of my experience.

He came to this disease with a lifetime of memorable achievements, during World War II and as a writer and

Washington celebrity. All of this was threatened as he attempted to extend his day and extend his life. Then his disease began to eat at the edges. The malignancy took over his life. Reading Alsop, there are times when I hear a common voice. He reports attitudes and feelings, concepts and ideas that I also have met along the way. He had more freedom of movement, but as with me, his days began to have a sameness. I know, for instance, just where I'll be two weeks from this very moment.

There is a lesson here. My friends urge me to do more. They try to motivate me. Offer their help. Invite me to all sorts of activities. It doesn't work.

Adventure will never again be part of my life. I must accept my limitations. I recall how I would send my heart attack patients home with instructions: "You can do things with your hands, but not your arms." Too much exertion at that second level.

Life is restricted to the finer moments. I must journey through books, converse by phone and letter, and view the ocean from my living room window, no longer able to let whim, or resolve, open up new worlds that a seventy-something may have missed.

*Dad was always a great finisher; he always advised
starting slowly and finishing well. He finished this race
well. But not typically. This time as he approached the
finish he didn't dive. He didn't reduce his consciousness to
the length of a stride. He slowed down and reached back.
He took my mother's hand, and he took all of our hands.
We all crossed the line together, fourteen abreast, stretched
out as far as the eye could see on either side. It was so
beautiful.*

TIM

Facing the Future

I RETURN AGAIN TO READING THORNTON
Wilder. He is certainly the novelist (*The
Bridge of San Luis Rey*) and playwright (*Our
Town*) for the dying person.

Can I pick the day I will die—or if I could,
should I? In *Our Town* Wilder lets his characters, or rather the Stage Manager, do just that. It turns
out, of course, that it makes little or no difference.

There are days when I feel it must come soon. The
weakness is worse, new pains appear, sleep is impossible.
Then that crisis passes. The doctors become optimistic.
We push it back a few months. This is a good day.

Before death made its threatening thrust I had many good days, many of them memorable. But Wilder sees this as of little importance. He allows the selection of a special day, but the Stage Manager knows better.

Wilder does also. His theme, as always, emphasizes the importance of every day. As I go though my last days I realize the truth of this. For one thing, I cannot fill days with the strength I have now—but more important, I want to be with the people who ordinarily fill my life.

Drama is not for us little people—yet it does come. There is the equilibrium I have reached with my family and avocations. And then it is disrupted by the knowledge of the cancer.

There is, of course, in my town only one satisfactory solution—my death.

I am therefore an actor, not a playwright—or perhaps I am both. My part is already written. When the biopsy was done it was inevitable. I used to die in every race, but in life I die only once. Now that is changed. I die seven days a week and twice on Wednesdays. It's now tragedy tomorrow, comedy tonight.

I AM SITTING IN THE SILENCE OF A QUAKER MEETING thinking about death and Canada geese. I am there because of death. My own. A few months back my doctor had suggested I had two months to live.

I brought this ominous concept of two months to live to the meeting, intending to grapple with it as best I could. I was new to Quaker meetings, but quiet seemed essential to meditation on death.

The first speaker had something to say about the Canada geese that were now populating the back of her property. I had put these two unlikely subjects together. The geese and death filled my mental side.

I could connect them. I had heard of a woman who lived in Minnesota. She had terminal cancer with a prognosis of two to three months more of life. One day as she stood on her porch she saw a squadron of Canada geese fly past. And she realized this would be the last time she would see Canada geese.

The geese alone provide for meditation.

The geese are beautiful. Geese are perfection. They carry out their programmed lifestyle without error. Their marvelous athletic ability is combined with a knowledge of where they are and pinpoint accuracy as to where they are going. They are nature at its best in action.

The Canada geese have no need to think this out. They will be geese no matter what. I, on the other hand, must be at all times consciously human. I must be a man. Sitting here I must be performing a human task.

The blind conformity of the geese compares to my agonizing pursuit of the self. Both of us move toward death and oblivion. The geese are blind to what's in store. I am all too conscious that I will join them. I must go the way of the grasshopper or the Canada goose.

And what of this death? It seems as I sit here that I must first accept what at this very moment seems inconceivable—that I will cease to be.

Nevertheless, I must make that small leap. I must capitulate to this necessity. This seems difficult (as it is for many) but is not in the same league as what is to follow.

Having accepted that death must come, I then must make the other decision: that God and immortality—all of the system beyond death—exists.

This is Kierkegaard's "Leap of Faith." The magnitude of this leap has escaped me until this moment. It is an awesome jump into an abyss. My ordinary world of geese and nature and all the life surrounding the meetinghouse is no more than "business, as usual." This is an unforgettable question—so much more daunting than Pascal's Wager: "You must either believe or not believe that God exists! Which will you do?"

Pascal, the intellectual, relied on the cold, impassive intellect. Kierkegaard, the melancholy dreamer, made demands no intellect would follow. "I believe because it's absurd" is the nonargument that falls into my mind.

The Wager comes up then. The geese, death, the

Wager, the Leap whirl and my mind is a kaleidoscope of different patterns. What does this equation offer me? At this time, does contemplation still have something to offer?

The answer is the breath of my experience. Contemplation is a response to experience. Here I'm facing new things, new ideas. But in a way I have been successful. Canada geese and death—my son the horse trainer would call that an odd exacta. But the child in me, or the minuscule element of William Blake, makes it work: "The Child's Toys & the Old Man's Reasons/Are the Fruits of the Two seasons"; "The child bangs on the wall until God answers the call."

I can see God or the Word.

We have been sitting for an hour. Others have risen up to comment. The geese represent order, they discipline their children, their world works. We could have our world work as well. We need not think of death—just the orderly management of our days until that death comes.

The geese are doing that superbly well and that is all they need to do. I have other obligations. Lead my life and then make my exit. And this is to be done under a certain dispensation that may punish or reward. It's designed to bring me to a final encounter.

· · ·

THE BOOK OF JOB HAS BEEN AN INEXHAUSTIBLE source of discussion for philosophers and theologians. It has provided material for poets and playwrights. But, as has always been the case, unless a person has had the Job experience, its meaning will remain elusive. Those who would have an inkling of what Job is going through must have gone through it themselves. And even those who write from personal experience cannot teach others.

There is a difference between "This will teach you" and "You will learn this." We can be taught a variety of things in a variety of ways, but things that we "learn" are direct, immediate, illuminating events that happen to us, where we are center stage. Things we are taught we know of; things we learn we know intimately.

The playwright William Gibson was on to this. He once wrote that every tragedy was a treasure to a writer. It goes without saying he meant real tragedies with real pain and real loss and real suffering. The creative artist almost always works from personal experience. What's best of all is when those learning experiences are no less than a litany of all the ills that man is heir to.

God is not teaching Job. Job is "learning" from Him and doing it quickly and decisively. Unless equivalent bad experiences have occurred to you, reading Job is no more than an intellectual exercise, a subject for debate perhaps as to its origin, or a continuing project of scriptural exegesis.

But not if you have been there yourself. Not if you have "learned" like Job. Then it is easy to understand the dialogue or to feel quite certain about your own interpretation. Anyone suffering through a painful terminal illness is no less than a modern-day Job. Treatments introduce new discomforts and new indignities. There is no joy. Like Job, the person appears to have been deserted.

In this hopeless and desperate situation it is well to remember the words of Ecclesiastes: "Everything is vanity." All Job's possessions, his farms, his livestock, his family, is vanity. And not only that, Job has already gone through the "times" catalogued by Ecclesiastes. But now look at it another way. Job has been made special. He has been singled out by God. Adversity has been heaped upon him. Only the best are subjected to such trials.

Suffering appears to be at issue, but it is not. Suffering is simply a way people learn that there is a life beyond suffering, beyond good and evil, beyond anything we can conceive. William James once said, "There are other and greater realities," and, in so many words, God says the same thing to the suffering Job. If we forget the happy ending, and we should, we can see that the question raised by the story of Job is immortality. The suffering that he undergoes is a pledge of the hereafter.

But, as I have said, you have to have been there to *learn* that.

ALTHOUGH 95 PERCENT OF AMERICANS SAY THEY believe in God, the Almighty is rarely the topic of our conversations. There are social reasons for this. Religion has been the cause of more rancor and strife than anything other than sex and money. We have learned to be wary about broaching the subject even with close friends.

Religion is also a private matter. William James defined it as "the feelings, acts, and experiences of individual men in their solitude, so far as they apprehend themselves to stand in relation to whatever they consider divine." In his *Varieties of Religious Experience* James said he set out first "to defend experience against philosophy as being the backbone of the world's religious life—I mean prayer, guidance and all that sort of immediately and privately felt, as against high and noble general views of our destiny and the world's meaning."

His second purpose was "to make the hearer or reader believe, what I myself invincibly believe, that although all the special manifestations may have been absurd (I mean its creeds and theories), yet the life of it as a whole is mankind's most important function."

While most believers would welcome that as a generous statement, many would not. About one half of Americans have accepted one of these creeds and a significant number of those attend services regularly. For them, agreeing that "God is" is not enough. For them, "God is precisely what I say He is."

James never reached that point himself. Yet few people have wrestled more deeply and more openly with the problem of God than he did. He was a scientist who knew science was not enough. He was a thinker who saw this as an area where thinking would fail. Religious experiences, he writes, "have no proper intellectual deliverance of their own but belong to a region deeper and more vital and practical than that which the intellect inhabits. For that reason they are indestructible by intellectual arguments and criticisms."

The Varieties of Religious Experience is a vast collection of these transforming and illuminating experiences occurring to people regardless of the catechism they support. The effects of these experiences are enormous. "The impressions and impulses and emotions and excitements we thence receive help us to live, they give invincible assurance of a world beyond the senses, they melt our hearts and communicate significance and value to everything and make us happy."

James himself, however, had difficulty aligning himself with a "higher power." "My position is simple," he writes, "I have no living sense of commerce with God. I envy those who have for I know that the addition of such a sense would help me greatly. The divine for my active life, is limited to impersonal and abstract concepts which as ideals, interest and determine me but do so but faintly in comparison with what a feeling of God might effect, if I had one."

Although he had never felt God's presence he accepted the testimony of those who had: "The whole line of testimony on this point is so strong I am unable to pooh-pooh it away." Nor was he able to dispense with his belief in personal immortality, which he expressed more strongly as he grew old, he said, "Because I am just getting fit for life."

When the psychologist Carl Stumpf wrote to James admitting his own religious state of mind and belief in immortality and a superhuman consciousness, James wrote back urging him to publish these confidences. "I think these states of mind, which are what people live by, are thoroughly normal; but the artificial rationalistic conscience of professional *gelehrten* [learned people] makes them so ashamed of the public expression of these inner faiths, that the literature of the world is getting too much weighted the other way; and, lacking examples of faith in minds whose intellects they respect, common people grow ashamed to have any faith of their own."

James emphasizes the similarity of the *feelings* and *conduct* that go with religious belief. Conduct is almost always the same. "Stoic, Christian and Buddhist saints are practically indistinguishable in their lives." As are the feelings: "an excitement of the cheerful, expansive, dynamogenic order which like any tonic, freshens our vital powers." And we see how this emotion "imparts endurance or a zest or a meaning, or enchantment and glory to the common objects of life."

What is the common intellectual basis of the various religions that spark these feelings and conduct? In James's analysis it consists of two parts:

1. *An uneasiness:* A sense that there is something wrong with us all; and
2. *Its solution:* We are saved from this wrongness by making proper connection with the higher power.

Along with the wrong part in us there is a better part, and this, the real us, is coterminous and continuous with more of the same quality that is operative in the universe outside of us and that we can keep in working touch with.

Conversations on such a vital subject as religion cannot be put on the back burner. They must be held. This need not be done in public, especially if we feel uncomfortable with the beliefs of those in our circle—but with ourselves certainly, and with those authors who have considered their faith as James did, with both his heart and his head. It is never too late to seek a transforming and illuminating religious experience.

Eventually every Christian has to ask himself or herself, "What do you think of Christ?"

Nevertheless, I think most of us put that question off. In some instances we presume we have already answered it and have not. We are living, as I was, in a reflex way, never totally committed to any particular philosophy of life.

My dead friends whose books I read tackled this problem and came up with varied answers. All were believers, but none seemed quite sure that he or she believed it. None, perhaps, had that peace beyond understanding. None could bring himself to the Pauline epigram: "Because it is incredible, I believe."

My feeling over the years is that there is a Christ for everyone. My Christ is not your Christ. I believe his agony was the Greek *agon*—a freely accepted, painful, and eventually death-dealing struggle with the self. The *agon* always has a closure and returns to peace and rest. It is never permanent. Athletes accept the *agon* repeatedly—when they cross the finish line they often have pushed beyond their limits. Then they are reborn and they rest.

What Christ says to me is not that we are all born sinners, but that we are all born *athletes.* We are born to play and play well (although most of us don't). We should not care about the outcome, because the aftermath will be filled with mirth and relaxation.

I may be totally off base, but I see in Christ the familiar athletic experience: the *askesis* in which one prepares for the approaching contest; the *agon* or the event; and the aftermath, where one is transformed by what has taken place.

In following Christ I repeat this *akesis,* this *agon* and its aftermath. I have my own liturgy, my own church, my own hierarchy. No matter that they differ from those of other Christians who follow their own Christ.

Santayana once wrote that within the Catholic church there are meadows where you can be alone and undisturbed. Just so. In the beginning we need the institutional church, Catholic or otherwise. But there comes a time when the church becomes unnecessary. As we grow in experience and wisdom we construct our own church. I have done that in part. I have left the herd. I no longer have to be taught how to survive in a world of barbarians. I can manage for myself.

Christ the athlete is a marvelous model. I can forget about original sin and concentrate on my original splendor. Life becomes a desperate struggle to return to the perfection of my birth. This is a Romantic notion found in most of the Romantic philosophers. The athlete is proof of the perfectibility of man. In the briefest of moments we see what we could and can be.

This is mere physical skill, you might say. But Santayana, in advocating sports for the college student, wrote that they prefigured perfection in other areas. Further, skill is unnecessary, and it is more than intelligence. "Effort is the measure of a man," writes William James. What makes the athlete is present in everyone. No special talent is necessary. Being all you can be is making actual only what is already potential within you.

Accepting Christ need not be accepting dogma. Accepting Christ may be an individual and idiosyncratic carrying out of the true and just and right way of life as I see it. In that each of us may honestly and fruitfully differ, just as the Christ of one Christian sect differs from that of another.

One thing is certain. Whatever I do I must do with all my might, and do it with the unmistakable belief that pain and death are necessary, if I am to become the person I was meant to be on the day I was born.

THERE ARE FEW OCCURRENCES IN THE BIBLE AS frustrating as the silence of Lazarus. He says nothing of his three days beyond the grave. He gives no answer to the question that came with the gift of consciousness: "After I die, what?" Whatever he learned on his trip to the other shore, we are never told.

There are some who think that Lazarus was distressed at being brought back. That he couldn't wait to die again. Being deprived of a beatific afterlife and returned to an imperfect world could be irritating. Further, someone who has seen the Promised Land plain might not be disposed toward what he considers idle chatter. Pascal and Aquinas, after their mystical experiences, saw great earthly achievements as of little value. Pascal made one pronouncement and let it go at that. Aquinas was not more communicative.

Perhaps this is best. Speculation on the hereafter can dim our enthusiasm for daily life. We could join the ranks of those who concentrate so much on a future of eternal bliss that they lose out on the marvelous, albeit transitory, joys that occur every day.

Yet few things in life are more interesting than what will come at its end. Death is a mystery that has defied the greatest minds in history. Geniuses have had their say and added nothing to the nothing we know. From antiquity much has been written, but nothing has dispelled our ignorance of what awaits us.

Most of us prefer to maintain that ignorance. In the face of death we are children. We react emotionally, and frequently our reactions are infantile. Rather than contemplate the possibilities we fly from their presence.

The late comedian Joe Williams used to tell a story about being pursued down a country road by a ghost. No matter how fast he ran the ghost was right behind him. Finally he could go no farther and collapsed, gasping, on the ground. The ghost then came to him and said, "That was quite a run we had, my friend." Williams, still gasping, looked up and answered, "It ain't nothing to the one we're going to have when I get my breath back."

If we dread death it is for two reasons. We have the fear that behind the curtain lies retribution for a lifetime of transgressions. We have the even greater fear that there is nothing there at all. Is death an irreversible and impersonal end to life's activities? Or is it a place we survive to be rewarded or punished for the lives we lead on earth? Or, and this is possibly the most threatening, will we live eternally the life and person we fashioned on earth?

Where then can we get reliable information about the

afterlife? The professionals in these matters are of little help. I mention Pascal and Aquinas, two acknowledged geniuses, but their revelations came not through their scholarship, but through their humanity. Not because of how they differed from common folk but because of qualities we all share.

So it is from ourselves and other ordinary human beings that we get inklings of what has been prepared for us. There are many people who had near-death experiences and have lived to tell us what they felt and saw. These voyagers in sacred space claim they have been dead and are back to report what it is like.

It is not enough to be on the verge of dying; not enough to be drawing your last breath, to arrive at this knowledge. One must have reached a level of reality that it represents an eternity to follow. These other-world travelers claim to have done just that. Not on their merits but just by happenstance. And the reports they bring back are not only accounts of that other world but also advice on how to live this life. They assure us of a life in the future, but even more they advise us on how to live in the present.

Over the centuries, this advice has changed. Those travelers out of the cosmos in the fourteenth century came back with a warning. Be good. God was like Santa

Claus. He was keeping a list and checking it twice. The medieval other-world voyagers came back as believers in law and order.

Our present-day travelers who have gone beyond space and time have a different message. The word is that we must be happy. Serve the Lord but be happy in His service. Love what you do and the people you do it with.

Emerson said this in another way. "The love that would be annihilated rather than be treacherous has already made death impossible." Love is also the message of Thornton Wilder's *The Bridge of San Luis Rey.* The closing passage of that classic novel on death is: "There is a land of the living and a land of the dead and the bridge is love, the only survival, the only meaning."

The important thing is not so much to be good as to be happy. Unfortunately it is much easier to be good than to be happy. Much easier to obey the decalogue than to be happy doing it. Happiness at its best is elusive. What we know of it seems twofold. First, it occurs during or after an action. Second, it is involved quite intimately with meaning. When we do something by which we know, feel, or sense meaning, happiness ensues.

Being good can result from nonaction. Passivity is a posture that prevents infractions of any regulations. Happiness, on the other hand, requires action. The good news that our salvation depends upon being happy may not be all that good. Joy and happiness do not come about by plan.

Satisfaction can come from a job well done, a temptation conquered, a seduction spurned. Joy is accompanied by tears and laughter and love. Sentiments to which satisfaction is a stranger.

Be happy! What a splendid order. How liberating. We are free, as we have always been, to pursue happiness in our own way, and thereby to pursue meaning, pursue love. In these experiences we can taste death. The near-death experience is no more than the full-life experience—those moments of the whole—me and a total relationship with myself or others or the world around me.

I could refer once again to Maslow's description of peak experience or the many varieties of religious experience described by William James. Happiness, joy, love are mystical experiences, which is to say that they cannot be totally accounted for in words. They are things that undoubtedly happen to us but defy our vocabulary. They defy precise definition.

J. M. Barrie once described death as "an awfully big adventure." It is an adventure from which none return. Logic fails us when we think on death. Logic does indeed tell us what is in store. "All men are mortal. You are a man. Therefore you are mortal." But the logic cannot tell us what follows that mortality. For that we must look inside ourselves for information. "The kingdom of heaven is within." How does it announce itself?

For some it comes through pushing the body and its limits. In *Sun and Steel,* Yukio Mishima describes this feeling. "My body would no longer tolerate intolerance. Thus for many a day I lead a life that others might well dismiss as a frenzied obsession. From the gymnasium to the fencing school, the school to the gymnasium. Ceaseless motion, ceaseless violent death—but I could not live without such mysteries. And needless to say within each mystery there lay a small imitation of death."

Dreams also give us a hint of what death is. Mircea Eliade tells of his dream of getting into a series of boats on the Ganges: "And suddenly I understood: everything became perfectly clear, extraordinarily clear and simple. Everything. Life, death and the meaning of existence." When he awoke, he determined not to forget what he had seen. A second later, he tells us, he had forgotten.

Perhaps a foretaste of what is in store is given to us in our rare moments of ecstasy when we feel wholeness and completion, and time becomes timeless. Nikolay Berdyayev wrote of a paradise that is not in the future, is not in time, but in eternity. "Eternity is attained in the actual moment—in the present which is an escape from time." This is a most important concept. Paradise on earth, in our time, would be the end of the creative process, of infinite striving, and consequently would mean boredom. What paradise then awaits us? The plot thickens. The mystery deepens. "After I die, what?" remains an inexhaustible topic.

Even if there are no answers, the result of such self-questioning gives some answers to another question: "Before I die, what?"

W E ARE IN A BEACH HOUSE IN REHOBOTH, Delaware. Taking our second family holiday of the summer. I am on a settee in the dining room. At the foot of the couch in the living room are ten or so Sheehans in laughing conversation. Plus the wonderful talk which I can vaguely hear. I can see a huge votive candelabra.

This is surely the way to go. The lights preceding me, praising the Lord. I am following a tradition that goes down through the centuries.

Today I have one or two of my usual falls. My weakness is increasing, but I know I'm on the right path.

This setting is like a funeral home. Without, thank God, the flowers. Better yet I could be Becket in a cathedral.

Your death was your final gift to us. It was filled with your love and courage, your brilliant intellect and wonderful humor. It was your total offering.

True to your philosophy, you gave it your all, fought the good fight, and truly went the distance with grace and bravery. You never let us know how hard the struggle was. My days are wonderful, you said. I have family and friends, my book to work on, the ocean to contemplate. You never told us what you must have felt: the pain, the frustration, and, ultimately, the loneliness of the dying process.

MARY JANE

A small room with the usual accoutrements of death. . . .

KENNETH TYNAN

A Blood Sport

THE WRITER HAS TO BE CAREFUL with figures of speech. It has been pointed out that the Bible is filled with riddles, puns, parables. The dying person cannot be faulted for using the same devices as Christ.

Death, as we may well learn in the hereafter, is a learning experience. Through this ordeal, or similar challenges, we keep growing until our last gasp.

I refuse to be limited in my understanding of what is going on in my psyche, my body in this trial. I have come to see death as a blood sport.

In Arles, France, 120,000 spectators watched this season's bullfights. A bullfight is likely to end with the killing of six bulls and, on occasion, the wounding or death of one of the fighters.

This is a blood sport and the people who live in Provence understand it. There is an implicit confrontation between life and death. This is a European characteristic. But it is not part of the American heritage. For the American it is the aesthetic. For the European the aesthetic is joined with risk. In Arles, the people find bullfights real and passionate.

This is not fiction. The death of the famous matador Manolete is as gripping as any novel. His final moments are the stuff of our greatest plays. In competition with a rising young rival, Luis Miguel Dominguin, he is urged by the public to persevere. This aging fighter presents a lonely figure. Seeing his face in photos is seeing what man can be. I am reminded of a five-year-old, upon seeing Ted Williams, telling her grandfather, "If God looked like a man, he would look like him."

Manolete presents a tragic figure as well. Bullfighters are killed—and most retire young. Eventually the fear becomes a reality. This day, Manolete is gored by the bull.

The final scene is theater in the round. The bare room. Manolete lying on the table, tourniquets in place to stanch the bleeding of the punctured thigh. Long intervals between speech. The usual accoutrements of death, a priest and extreme unction.

The bullfighter is also a metaphor. I think of dying as a blood sport, similar to the bullfight. The bullfight brings the moment of truth. It is the ballet of death.

Of the nine arts, the philosopher Paul Weiss thought the ballet was the most important. In the performance there is a play, a story, there is music, and there is dance. This brings us a complete picture of the protagonist.

Going face-to-face with cancer can be looked at as my blood sport. This coming together offers me a chance at a new role. Cancer, like the bull, is death, and I am defending myself, dancing with death, creating this beautiful aesthetic. The blood sports show that death is not defeat. Like Manolete my role is to make this a classic, frozen picture of the end passage of life.

For me this is all in my imagination. I am not in Arles or Pamplona. I don't go out and run with the bulls. In reality my day doesn't include putting on my "suit of lights" and practicing passes with my *muleta*. None of these things occurs.

Instead I awaken in the morning and discover that my left leg is paralyzed. Or rather, I forget that my left leg is paralyzed. It wears off later, but not before I almost fall on the way to the bathroom. But in my mind I am still Manolete. Like him, I shoulder my cape, hear the trumpets, and go into battle.

My cancer progresses, albeit slowly. Indeed the slowness of it surprises. I had long since expected the worst. I am becoming embarrassed that I am still alive. In much the same way it most likely occurs to bullfighters or their counterparts, the gunslingers who once populated our West.

The cancer, like the bull, advances, retreats, charges with élan. It draws blood, staggers me, follows me looking to administer, as I do, the coup de grâce.

Unknowing, this magnificent animal represents the forces of nature that would bring us down. Together with the errors of nature in my own body, it leads to inevitable dissolution.

Each day brings new assaults on my body. I stand in the center of the arena, beset by not only the cares of the day, but also my inability to fulfill them. My lounge chair is my choice of place for the morning. My exercise routines—running, cycling, swimming—are beyond me. The stairs have become Heartbreak Hill.

Unlike Manolete, the bullfighter who was dispatched quite rapidly, my disease has been slow. My life is not over in an afternoon. I find the analogy, therefore, difficult to make. Yet in many ways it is quite the same. A small room with the usual accoutrements of death.

I read of Manolete's death and see mine in the coming.

TODAY I EXPERIENCED THE SUDDEN ONSET OF high neck pain. My Percocet gave me some relief. However, two hours later I felt the return of a severe occipital headache. This may well be how I am to go.

I recall the famous Boston physician Soma Weiss saying to his medical students, "I am having a cerebral hemorrhage," collapsing, and then dying. This appears to be the same thing.

The pain is not effort-induced, but then neither is the ecchymosis of my arms. I worried about my platelets, apparently without cause. Still, like many other episodes, this may not mean anything.

As it is, I am alone in the house on a weekend, when everyone could be available to bid me good-bye. And God, I do feel as if this is the hour. I wonder how this time was selected.

What last words do I have? Will they be "How beautiful," like that twenty-one-year-old woman—or will it refer to the end of a perfect race? I wait for what comes

next. The second Percocet is not as effective. Thirty minutes and I still have pain.

Today the priest came. I was dozing and
found myself looking up into the face of Father
Brady, our longtime pastor at the parish
church.

Brady is a burly, middle-aged Irishman, a mesomorph
with thick, wide wrists and still fit enough to have the
gregarious nature that is needed in my instance.

He is a very kind, soft-spoken man who began his visit
by saying, "I'm not here to help you with your theological
problems, George, but with your relationship with God."

Particular religions demand particular temperaments. I
would not have thought that Brady and I would hit it off,
but Brady reminded me of Toynbee . . . he wanted me to
have "a maximum of religion and a minimum of theology."

I saw him on his deathbed. He was not alert, he was panting, starting to withdraw, to pull away. But inside I sensed a focus and an intent that he was trying to accomplish something. I went home and the next morning I got news of his death. My emotion was very curious. It was more awe and respect. I said to myself, Oh my God—he did it, he did it. He accomplished it—he died the graceful death. He reunited the family that had been torn over the years. I think his death was the final and most glorious achievement of his great life. To the list of his many attributes, we can now add courage.

PETER

Epilogue

THESE WERE THE LAST SENTENCES my father dictated to me. His concentration gone, he didn't even have the strength to use a walker. We moved a hospital bed into the living room overlooking the ocean, and as he weakened we had to lift him from bed to chair.

A few days before he died, Father Brady, who was visiting him and had just administered the Blessing of the Sick, pulled my mother and me aside. What he said was very comforting: "Mary Jane, George is at peace. He received the Blessing with tears not of guilt, but of joy. A true communion with God. He's ready to go . . . he just wants the family to accept that." Dad was worried about extra measures like IV feeding requiring a visit to the "Hospital"—the very word terrified him.

Family surrounded him from then on and as my brother Andrew recounted, "The pain humbled him and sweetened him." For one who decried sentimentality, Dad frequently became teary-eyed with all his children down the stretch. Nothing but praise for each one; each an "experiment of one" (as he would say in his talks). For my mother he would say, "Your mother and I have had the best two months of our lives," although he would whisper to me, when she might be stingy with the painkillers, "Your mother is becoming Nurse Ratchet!"

The end came a few days after Father Brady spoke of Dad's acceptance of death. A bowel blockage caused by the morphine hardening the stool had Dad in real pain. Remedies included more painkillers. It was Friday. He lapsed into a sleep that worked its way into Sunday night. A visiting nurse told us he might die within twenty-four hours. Apparently, the sleep was caused by the body breaking down, not the medication. Dad in a dark blue turtleneck, lying under the covers with a handcloth on his brow, was looking like he did during his days in the Lenox Hotel recovering from a Boston Marathon.

Some say life isn't fair. Although Dad died the next

morning with the family around the bed, Mom was not there. This "domestic athlete," as Dad once wrote of her, was out at 9:00 A.M. running errands. While all of us were in tears around the bed I noticed Mom parking the car in front of the house.

No makeup man in Hollywood could have disguised our sorrow, but I said, "We can't let her know until she gets up to the living room." I ran down and took her groceries. In front of me she began walking up the stairs. Her shrinking figure made me realize her age and how long they had been together.

When she reached the top and entered the room she saw the sad faces . . . and she knew. Startled, she threw up her hands in front of her face, exclaiming plaintively, "Let me have him." Breaking through us, she ran to his bedside, grabbing his head and smothering him with kisses. "I love you so, we had such a wonderful life."

A Beautiful End. I tell it to you because stories of love should not be hidden.

—*George Sheehan III*

About the Author

DR. GEORGE SHEEHAN was a cardiologist, writer, record-setting runner, and mentor to thousands. At age fifty he set the world record of 4:45 in his age group for the mile. At sixty-one, he set his personal marathon record of 3:01, an amazing time for a runner even half that age. He ran more than sixty marathons and wrote seven books, including *Dr. Sheehan on Running*, *Running and Being*, and *Personal Best*. Dr. Sheehan was the father of twelve children and lived with his wife, Mary Jane, at the New Jersey Shore. He died in November 1993 at the age of seventy-four.